THE LITTLE FLOWER

BOOKS BY MARY FABYAN WINDEATT

A Series of Twenty Books

Stories of the Saints for Young People ages 10 to 100

THE CHILDREN OF FATIMA
And Our Lady's Message to the World

THE CURÉ OF ARS
The Story of St. John Vianney, Patron Saint of Parish Priests

THE LITTLE FLOWER
The Story of St. Therese of the Child Jesus

PATRON SAINT OF FIRST COMMUNICANTS
The Story of Blessed Imelda Lambertini

THE MIRACULOUS MEDAL
The Story of Our Lady's Appearances to St. Catherine Labouré

ST. LOUIS DE MONTFORT
The Story of Our Lady's Slave, St. Louis Mary Grignion De Montfort

SAINT THOMAS AQUINAS
The Story of "The Dumb Ox"

SAINT CATHERINE OF SIENA
The Story of the Girl Who Saw Saints in the Sky

SAINT HYACINTH OF POLAND
The Story of the Apostle of the North

SAINT MARTIN DE PORRES
The Story of the Little Doctor of Lima, Peru

SAINT ROSE OF LIMA
The Story of the First Canonized Saint of the Americas

PAULINE JARICOT
Foundress of the Living Rosary & The Society for the Propagation of the Faith

SAINT DOMINIC
Preacher of the Rosary and Founder of the Dominican Order

SAINT PAUL THE APOSTLE
The Story of the Apostle to the Gentiles

SAINT BENEDICT
The Story of the Father of the Western Monks

KING DAVID AND HIS SONGS
A Story of the Psalms

SAINT MARGARET MARY
And the Promises of the Sacred Heart of Jesus

SAINT JOHN MASIAS
Marvelous Dominican Gatekeeper of Lima, Peru

SAINT FRANCIS SOLANO
Wonder-Worker of the New World and Apostle of Argentina and Peru

BLESSED MARIE OF NEW FRANCE
The Story of the First Missionary Sisters in Canada

THE LITTLE FLOWER

THE STORY OF SAINT THERESE OF THE CHILD JESUS

By
Mary Fabyan Windeatt

Illustrated by
Gedge Harmon

TAN BOOKS AND PUBLISHERS, INC.
Rockford, Illinois 61105

Imprimi Potest: ✠ Ignatius Esser, O.S.B.
Abbot of St. Meinrad's Abbey

Nihil Obstat: Gabriel Verkamp, O.S.B., S.T.D., Ph.D.
Censor Deputatus

Imprimatur: ✠ Joseph E. Ritter, D.D.
Archbishop of Indianapolis

First published in 1944, as "A Grail Publication," at St. Meinrad, Indiana, under the title *Little Queen: (The Story of) St. Therese of The Child Jesus.*

ISBN: 0-89555-413-5

Library of Congress Catalog Card No.: 90-71829

Printed and bound in the United States of America.

TAN BOOKS AND PUBLISHERS, INC.
P.O.Box 424
Rockford, Illinois 61105

1991

For My Mother

CONTENTS

INTRODUCTION

You have heard of me. You have seen my pictures and medals. Perhaps you have even said some prayers in my honor. After all, God has made me known to children as well as to older people. And why? So that I may tell them about the Little Way I followed while on earth, the Little Way that led me to love Him with all my heart. What if I have been dead since September 30, 1897? I still work for God. I still bring Him thousands of souls every day, souls who were afraid of Him at first, afraid of His Will, but now are eager to do everything He asks just because I showed them how to love Him.

I do this work mainly through a book I wrote a short while before I died. This book, *The Story of a Soul,* was written in French, my native language. Today, however, *The Story of a Soul* has been translated into thirty-five other languages, and maybe one of the English copies is in your home or at school. I hope so, for this book tells how I became a saint. It will help you to become a saint, too.

When you are older you will read *The Story of a Soul.* In the meantime, here is another book for you to read. It will tell you about me—a French girl who was called Marie Frances Therese Martin in Baptism and who later received another name: Saint Therese of the Child Jesus and of the Holy Face.

CHAPTER 1

THE BABY OF THE MARTIN FAMILY

PAPA was a watchmaker and had a rather long name — Louis Joseph Aloysius Stanislaus Martin. Mama's was much shorter — Zelie Marie Guerin. They were married on July 13, 1858, in the church of Notre Dame in Alencon, France. Papa was about thirty-five years old at the time, Mama twenty-six. A few people were afraid that the marriage was a mistake. You see, they were remembering those days long ago when Papa thought he had a vocation to be a monk. They also remembered that Mama once tried to enter the religious life, too—as a Sister of Saint Vincent de Paul.

"Louis Martin and Zelie Guerin are far too holy to live in the world," these people told one another. "Each would be better off in some monastery."

But this was not so. God did not want Papa or Mama to live in the cloister. He wanted them to live in the world. He wanted them to have many children and to teach these little ones the beauties of the Catholic faith. So it was that they married each other, that thirteenth day of July in the year 1858, and settled down to a quiet life in Alencon.

The first child God sent my parents was a girl. She was called Marie Louise in Baptism, although from the start Papa just called her Marie—which is the French form for Mary.

'We'll give each of our little ones the first name of Marie," he said. "Even the boys. In this way they'll all be consecrated to the Blessed Virgin."

It was a fine thought, and one with which Mama readily agreed. She had a very high opinion of Papa, and not a day passed that she did not thank God for giving her such a fine husband. How kind he was! And how hard he worked at his watch-making so that she might have a comfortable home! Truly, there was no better man in Alencon, in all France, than Louis Joseph Aloysius Stanislaus Martin!

As time passed, my parents prayed very hard that God would send them a little boy. They were anxious to have a son to give to the priesthood. But the next three babies were all girls: Marie Pauline, Marie Leonie, Marie Helen. It did seem as though the many prayers for a son, "a little missionary," would never be answered. Then one fine day Marie Joseph Louis came to gladden the hearts of all.

"Here's our priest!" said Papa delightedly.

Alas! The new baby lived only five months. Then

God called him to Heaven. The same thing happened with Marie Joseph John Baptist—the sixth child to come into our home. This little brother lived to be eight months old. Then he died, too.

Poor Papa! Poor Mama! They were deeply afflicted at the loss of their two little sons. But they loved God in a really honest way, which means that they loved His Will and trusted it more than their own. Therefore, they did not grieve long. Besides, faith told them that they had given new saints to love God in Heaven.

"The boys will pray for us," Papa said. "Just think! They went to God without one sin on their souls!"

Presently another girl was born in our house—Marie Celine. The next year came one more—Marie Melanie Therese. This little one lived only a short time. Then death came again as God called to Himself the fourth child in our family: five-year-old Marie Helen.

The neighbors were shocked at all the sorrow which came to our house. "Four children dead out of eight!" they said, sadly shaking their heads. "Really, it would be better if these little ones had never been born. Then their parents would have been spared a good deal of pain."

"No, no!" Mama would protest. "My children are not lost to me. Life is short. We shall meet again in Heaven."

"And we still have Marie, Pauline, Leonie and Celine to cheer us up," Papa would put in, comfortingly. "My business is prospering, too. Why should we complain?"

Everyone marveled at the wonderful way in which Papa and Mama accepted these fresh trials. Death had called four times in twelve years, yet the Martin house was still a cheerful place. So was the shop where Papa worked at his trade of watchmaker and jeweler. It was a pleasure to visit either one.

Time passed, and presently it was the year 1873. Marie and Pauline, students at the Visitation convent in Le Mans, were home in Alencon for their Christmas vacation. Late on the night of January 2, Papa went upstairs to the little room where they were sleeping.

"Wake up, children!" he cried excitedly. "I have some news for you!"

The girls sat up with a start, blinking at the light from Papa's lamp. What had happened? Why was their father standing in the doorway with such a big smile on his face?

"What is it, Papa?" asked Marie anxiously. "Mama's not sick again?"

A dozen questions were on Pauline's tongue, but Papa gave her no chance to ask them.

"No, Marie. Mama's all right. And you have a new sister now—a beautiful little girl!"

Yes—it was January 2, 1873, and God had sent me to earth at last—to the wonderful Christian home of Louis Martin, watchmaker of Alencon!

"PAPA, WHAT'S THE BABY'S NAME?"

Of course Marie and Pauline found it hard to go to sleep after Papa's visit. They asked each other many questions about me. For instance, was I a healthy baby? Would I stay with them or go to Heaven like the other little sisters and brothers? What would Papa and Mama call me? When would I be baptized? Who would be my godmother?

"Marie, I think you'll be chosen," said Pauline suddenly. "After all, you're the oldest—thirteen next month. I'm only eleven."

Marie smiled. To be godmother of the new little sister! That would be wonderful!

"Oh, I hope so," she said softly. "I've never been a godmother in my whole life."

So it came to pass that on January 4, when I was two days old, a little procession set out from our house and made its way through the snowy streets to the church of Notre Dame. Our maid, Louise, carried me in her arms, well wrapped in blankets. Then came Papa, with Marie and Pauline each hanging on an arm. There were also some neighbors and friends.

"Papa, tell us again what the baby is going to be called," said Marie. "I'm so excited about being her godmother that I'm not just sure."

Papa laughed heartily. "Her name is a nice one, child. Marie Frances Therese." Then the happy light died out of his eyes as he gave a quick glance at the wintery sky.

"Dear God, please leave this child with us!" he whispered. "In the Name of Thy Son, Jesus Christ!"

There was good reason for Papa to be anxious about me. In the days following my Baptism, I fell ill and it seemed likely that God soon would take me to Himself in Heaven.

"The only way that this child can be saved is to give her to a good nurse," said the doctor. "One who lives in the country. Perhaps with proper food and plenty of fresh air and sunshine, the baby will get strength enough to live."

Poor Mama! She did not want to be parted from me, yet she agreed to do whatever the doctor thought best. There was a farm woman she knew, Rose Taillé, who might take care of me for a few months. She had been very successful in nursing other sick children. Perhaps she could help me, too.

Rose Taillé wasn't sure about this. The day Mama brought her into Alencon to have a look at me, the good-natured woman gave a great sigh. She had never seen such a poor little scrap of humanity. Why, I was nothing but skin and bones! And so pale!

"I'll do my best," she told Mama. "But I can promise you nothing, Madame. Ah, what a sickly little mite we have here! Only prayers will save her, I'm thinking."

Mama nodded. There would be plenty of prayers —to Saint Joseph, to the Blessed Virgin, to all the saints. Oh, how she would pray for me! And Papa, too.

So Rose took me out into the country, pausing frequently on the journey to see if I was still alive.

She was a little worried about this new responsibility. She had four children of her own to care for, and it was necessary to help her husband with the farm work, too. Perhaps she shouldn't have taken me with her. If I died, people might blame her.

But I did not die. God heard the fervent prayers which Papa and Mama offered for my recovery, and at Rose's house I became a totally different child. This was not because the good woman had any luxuries to give me. On the contrary, she had very little time to spend on my care. Because there was no proper carriage, she would put me in a wheelbarrow filled with hay and take me out to where she and her husband were working. Sometimes I was left alone under a tree. At others, Rose put the wheelbarrow in the sun.

"The little one is too pale," she said. "Maybe the sunshine will help her to grow strong."

I did grow strong and brown. In a few months there was no longer any danger that I would die. Rose was very proud, and one May day she took me home to show Mama how I had grown. Why, I weighed fourteen pounds!

"Therese is going to be all right, Madame," she said thankfully. "And I think I can leave her with you, now that she's nearly five months old."

Mama was so happy. "Rose, how can I thank you?" she cried. "You saved my little girl's life!"

Rose smiled shyly as she put me into Mama's

arms. "I have to go to the market now," she said. "It's the day for selling butter, and I'm late."

Of course I could not understand what Rose was saying, but it did not take long for me to realize that she had left me in a stranger's arms. At once I started to cry. Nothing could make me stop. As time passed Mama became frightened. She tried to comfort me, to sing little songs, to rock me to sleep. I wasn't interested. I wanted Rose, no one else. Finally Mama called the maid.

"Louise, what am I going to do? Therese will make herself sick with all this crying!"

Louise peered down at me. I was screaming at the top of my lungs, and my face was a deep and angry red.

"Do you really want my opinion, Madame?"

"In Heaven's name, yes! None of my other children ever acted like this."

Louise smiled. "It's simple, Madame. The child wants Rose. She won't stop crying unless we take her to her."

"But Rose is selling butter at the market!"

"She could still look after the baby, Madame. And she'd be pleased if we told her how the little one misses her."

Poor Mama! She didn't want to let go of me but there was nothing else to do. "All right," she said sadly. "Take Therese down to the market, Louise. But if she still keeps on crying, what shall we do then?"

There was no need for Mama to worry about this. As soon as Louise and I arrived at the market, where women from the farms outside Alencon were selling their butter, I began to smile. Then I laughed and laughed, for my eyes had caught sight of Rose. I stretched out my arms happily. This was what I had wanted all the time—*my mother!*

I stayed at the market until noon, happy and contented as Rose and her friends sold their butter. A few people asked questions about me as I lay quietly in my good friend's arms.

"Rose, I didn't know you had such a little girl as this one," they remarked. "And she has fair hair. I thought all your children were dark."

Rose laughed. "Oh, the child isn't mine," she said.

"Then whose is she?"

"She belongs to the Martin family, Lord bless her! And good as gold she is, too — at least when I'm looking after her!"

CHAPTER 2

PAPA'S LITTLE QUEEN

PRESENTLY the doctor announced that it was no longer necessary for Rose Taillé to look after me. I was strong and well and could return home to Alencon permanently. Mama was delighted at the news, and Papa also. He began to call me by a pet name, "Little Queen," and never tired of holding me in his arms. One day he told Mama he was going to build a swing for me in the back yard.

"*A swing?* But Therese is too young for that!" cried Mama. "She's only eighteen months old."

Papa just laughed. "The little one will love a swing," he said. "Then she can fly through the air like an angel."

Mama had no use for such nonsense, but finally she had to agree that Papa had been right. Her little Marie Frances Therese liked nothing better than to be taken out to the swing. One day she wrote a letter to my two big sisters, Marie and Pauline, who were at boarding school in Le Mans.

"Therese acts just like an older child. There is no danger that she will let go the rope. When the swing is not going high enough, she calls out to us. Then we tie a cord in front to keep her from falling off."

Mama was anxious that her five children should grow up to be good Catholics. She taught us prayers when we were still very small, and took great pleasure in telling us about God and Heaven. One day, when I was about three years old, I looked at her seriously.

"Mama, I want you to die. And Papa, too."

Mama stared at me in shocked amazement. "What a thing to say, Therese! Don't you love me? Don't you love your good father who does so many nice things for you?"

I nodded. "Yes, but I want you to go to Heaven. People have to die before they can do that."

Papa was very amused at my remark. "Therese is going to be a clever girl when she grows up," he said. "And she's going to be pretty, too. Aren't you, Little Queen?"

Mama shook her head. "You'll spoil the child if you're not careful," she warned. "She has lots of pride."

"*Pride?* This baby?"

"That's right. Therese, tell Papa what you said to me the other day when I offered you a penny."

I climbed onto my father's lap. "Mama said I could have a penny if I kissed the ground," I explained. "But I didn't want the penny that much, Papa. I wouldn't kiss the ground for anything!"

At the expression on my face Papa burst into hearty laughter. "Now I know why I call you my Little Queen," he said. "You act just like a real one. And I love you for it."

Before her marriage, Mama had learned how to make beautiful lace. She still kept busy with this work and employed several women to help her. They labored in their own homes and brought in their pieces of lace at regular intervals. Mama put together sections in attractive patterns and many people thought that there was no better lace to be found anywhere. They gave Mama so many orders that finally Papa decided to stop being a watchmaker and jeweler. He would help Mama with the lace business, which was growing every day. As a result, we soon had quite a lot of money in the bank. This was a good thing, for it allowed us to help the poor in many ways. But it also put strange ideas in some people's heads.

"Louis Martin is becoming quite an important man," they told one another. "Probably his daughters will be able to go into real society when they grow up."

"Yes," was the answer. "They are pretty girls. They won't have any trouble in finding themselves good husbands."

Alas! These people never dreamed that God would call us children to a very different kind of life. They did not know that already Pauline was thinking of becoming a nun; that I, loving this big sister so much, had decided to be a nun, too. Of course I did not understand what this really meant, but still I felt that all things were possible for me. Wasn't I Papa's Little Queen? Of course!

Time passed. Marie finished her studies at the Visitation convent in Le Mans and came home. She was fifteen years old, and it was decided that she could teach Celine how to read and write. This little sister was six years old and my favorite playmate. We had never been separated. Now, however, Celine was taken away for lessons and I had to be alone for hours at a time. This nearly broke my heart.

"Please let me have lessons, too!" I begged Mama. "Let me sit in the room when Marie teaches Celine."

Mama thought I was too small. She explained that reading and writing are not meant for little girls of three. Seeing my tears, Papa settled things by saying I could stay in the room if I was very quiet and did not disturb my sisters. I promised eagerly, and my love for Papa reached new heights. He was so good! He would do anything to make his Little Queen happy!

Marie was not too pleased when she heard that I was to be present at Celine's lessons. Some days she shut the door of her room, knowing I was too small to open it myself and that my pride would never let me ask for help. But this did not keep me back. Whenever I found Marie's door shut, I would lie down outside, not in tears, but very solemn and hurt. I knew that finally someone would come along and find me. They would be very touched at my loneliness. They would make a big fuss over me and say what a pity it was that Marie was so hard-hearted. But this plan succeeded only a few times, for one day Marie told me it was not right to act in such a way.

"You are grieving the Little Jesus," she said reproachfully.

I was shocked. I had no wish to grieve the Little Jesus. I wanted to do just those things which would please Him.

After this I often thought of the things I had done which must have hurt the Little Jesus. There were many of these, and most occurred because of my temper and my pride. For instance, much as I loved Celine, I sometimes grew cross with her when we were playing and she did not let me have my way. I would slap and push her. I would stamp my foot. Then there was the dreadful day when I had been rude to Papa. While I was swinging in the garden, he had called out to me to come and give him a kiss.

"You'll have to come and get it yourself," I replied, and swung higher. A few seconds later I realized what I had done. Instantly I stopped the swing, got down, and with many tears and sobs ran after Papa. Seeing that I was sorry, he smiled and told me not to worry any more. Wasn't I his Little Queen? Weren't we the best of friends?

There was another black mark for me to remember. One morning as Mama was going to Mass, she stopped by my bed to see how I was. It was very early, and I pretended to be asleep so that she would not try to kiss me. Marie guessed my deceit, however.

"I'm sure Therese is only pretending," she said. "She's really awake, Mama."

Hearing this, I hid under the sheet. "I don't want anyone to look at me," I said crossly. "I want to be left alone."

This was acting like a spoiled child, and Mama was very disappointed in me. She told me so and then went downstairs without kissing me good-bye. As had happened before, grief filled my heart an instant later, and I ran after her to say that I was sorry. Of course she forgave me at once, just as Papa had done, but such kindness could not alter the fact that I had been bad. I should have to change my ways if I wanted to go to Heaven.

When one is three years old, one's thoughts are very simple. In a little while I had arrived at a solution of my problem. A saint is a person who loves God and always says "Yes" to Him. Well, that would be my plan. I would always say "Yes" to God. Whenever He suggested that I obey my parents and sisters, be willing and cheerful about the house, I would say "Yes." It would be hard sometimes, of course, but I was such a little thing that God would help me over the rough places.

No one learned of my new thought, and at first there seemed to be little change in me. I still liked having my own way. I still liked having pretty clothes and other nice things. Then one day I showed how very selfish I really was. Leonie came to Celine and me with a big basket of playthings which she had outgrown.

"Here," said this big sister, setting down the basket, "you two are still children. I'm going to let you have all these old toys. Since you're the older, Celine, you may have first choice."

Celine's blue eyes looked long and lovingly at the sudden wealth. A doll, doll clothes, pieces of colored silk and many other wonderful things were in the basket. Finally she picked up a ball.

"Could I have this, Leonie?"

"Of course. Now it's your turn, Therese."

I spent no time in making a choice. I reached out both arms and snatched the basket to my heart. "I choose everything!" I cried, and with an air of triumph marched out of the room.

Shortly after my fourth birthday, Mama reeived a letter from Le Mans. It told of the death of her sister, a holy nun in the Visitation convent there. Naturally Mama was saddened by this news. She and Sister Mary Dosithée had always been very dear friends. Now they would never see each other again in this world.

"Children, I want you to pray to your aunt for a very special intention," Mama told us one day. "I'm sure she is in Heaven now. She will be glad to make me happy by answering your prayers."

Celine and I obeyed, as did Marie and Pauline and Leonie. I said "Yes" to God many times, wondering what the special intention could be. Perhaps it had something to do with the sadness in Mama's eyes, I thought, for though I was only four years old I knew a change had come over our happy home. Papa no longer smiled as in the old days. The maid, Louise, often cried when she thought no one was watching.

Presently Mama went to visit her brother in Lisieux. This brother, Isidore Guerin, was a very wise man. He owned a chemist's shop, and people often came to him with their troubles. How I hoped he could help Mama with hers! But when she returned to Alencon, I knew that Uncle Isidore had not been able to do anything.

"What is it?" I wondered sadly. "What is wrong with Mama?" Then Papa solved the mystery for us. Mama was sick, very sick. And she was suffering great pain.

"Ask God to cure her!" he begged. "Offer Him all your actions during the day. Don't let an hour go by without making some sacrifice for our great intention."

Celine and I prayed very hard. Marie had given each of us some beads which could be moved forward on their chain. She had brought these to us from the Visitation convent in Le Mans. Celine and I became very busy with these beads. Each time we made a sacrifice, or offered some very special prayer, we pushed forward a bead.

"How hard we are praying for Mama!" Celine said one day. "Do you think God is going to hear us?"

I nodded. Long ago I had heard Pauline say that no prayer goes unanswered. In a little while God would give Mama good health. There was no need to worry.

In the middle of June Mama decided to make a pilgrimage to Lourdes. Marie, Pauline and Leonie were to accompany her. They would beg the Blessed Virgin to grant our mother the gift of health. Naturally Celine and I wanted to visit the beautiful shrine, too. We could have shed bitter tears at not being invited, but Papa's sorrowful face was too much for us. We could not add to his grief.

"We'll pray for you at home, Mama," said Celine earnestly. "The Blessed Virgin will hear us."

Mama gave her an affectionate smile, then turned to me. "God bless you, darling," she murmured. "I'll be back in a little while."

The next few days were lonely ones. Papa spent long hours in church, while Celine and I continued to make sacrifices and offer many prayers for the intention so close to our hearts. On the day of Mama's return, we went with Papa to the station in great excitement. Surely our prayers and sacrifices had not been in vain! Surely we could have a happy home once more! But a blow awaited us. Mama was going to die!

"Don't grieve," she told us tenderly. "The Blessed Virgin has said to me as she said to Bernadette: 'I will make you happy not in this world but in the next.' "

CHAPTER 3

LEARNING TO LIVE WITHOUT OUR DEAR MAMA

THE next few weeks were full of pain and strangeness. Because Papa did not wish that Celine and I should witness Mama's great sufferings, we were sent to a neighbor's house each day. This made us feel like little exiles, particularly on those mornings when we did not have enough time to say our prayers before leaving. When we shyly told the neighbor lady about this, she led us to a large room.

"You can say your prayers here, little ones. No one will bother you."

Now Celine and I felt even lonelier. Mama or Papa had always helped us with our prayers. We had never had to say them by ourselves. After a little while, however, the distressing visits ended. It seemed that Mama was going to die any minute. Since she wished to have all her children with her at the last, Celine and I were allowed to stay at home all day.

On August 26 Papa went to get the priest. It was time for the Last Sacraments. I knelt in a corner of Mama's room and watched her being prepared for the mysterious journey to Heaven. Papa and my sisters were crying bitterly, but there were no tears in my eyes. Two days later, when Mama was gone from us forever, it was still the same. Sorrow made my heart stiff, and I could not cry. Nor could I unburden myself to anyone. It seemed as though I could only look and wonder at the dreadful sadness which had entered our home.

"The baby is too small to understand what's happened," said someone. "Poor little thing! What's going to become of her now?"

I made no effort to explain how I really felt, to describe the choked feeling in my heart. I was silent, too, when I came across Mama's coffin in the hall. Someone had left it there, and for several minutes I stood before this long and narrow box in quiet thought. What a gloomy thing it was! How sad and lonely!

When Papa brought us home from the funeral, we five girls looked at one another silently. There was no need to say it. The house was not the same with Mama gone. We were not the same either, dressed in new, unfamiliar black. Our maid, Louise, was overcome with compassion at the sight of our grief-stricken faces and put her arms tenderly about Celine and me.

"Poor little children!" she murmured. "You don't have a mother any more!"

At this Celine burst into tears and ran towards Marie. "You're my mother!" she sobbed. "Marie, say you'll be my mother!"

I was tempted to imitate my little sister's action. Then I looked at Pauline. Perhaps she also would like a little daughter? Maybe she was feeling sad because Celine had not chosen her? Slowly I advanced toward my second oldest sister. As she bent to caress me, I put my head against her heart.

"Pauline, *you* will be my mother," I said softly.

Naturally Marie and Pauline agreed to take Mama's place as best they could. They had now completed their education at the convent in Le Mans and would be able to stay at home. They would look after Leonie, Celine and me. However, Papa was afraid that the work of running the house and of guiding three little sisters would be too much for girls still in their teens. After due thought, he decided to move from Alencon to Lisieux. Mama's brother, Isidore Guerin, lived here. He and his wife, our beloved Aunt Celine, would be glad to help the two older girls in their new duties. Accordingly, a house was purchased in Lisieux and in November of that same year, 1877, we said farewell to Alencon.

What a sad group we made, that day we left for our new home! It was a real sorrow, particularly for Marie and Pauline, to say good-bye to our friends and neighbors, to visit the graves of Mama and our little brothers and sisters for the last time. But I did not cry, although my heart was heavy as I looked at the front stairs. How well I knew these stairs! When I had been learning to walk, I would climb up on one step, then call "Mama." If my good mother did not answer "Yes, darling," I would go no farther. Well, never again should I hear that dear voice encouraging me in my little troubles. Never again, at least in this world, could I take refuge in her arms.

I was not too sad at leaving Alencon, however, for a child of four loves change. When we arrived in Lisieux, our Aunt Celine and her two little girls, Jane and Marie, were waiting for us on the steps of their house. They gave us a warm welcome and invited us to stay with them that first night. The next morning we went to see our new home, *Les Buissonnets,* which corresponds to the English phrase "a wooded estate" and which can be correctly called *The Elms.* It was outside the town, and there were many trees and flowers. I fell in love with *The Elms* at once, although Aunt Celine did not guess it.

"Therese is so quiet," she told Pauline. "Poor little thing! She must be lonely for her mother."

It was true. I was to be a sad and solemn child for many years, for Mama's death had caused an enormous change in me. Overnight I had become shy and timid, and it took very little to make me cry.

After a few weeks at *The Elms,* Papa decided

to send Leonie and Celine to the Benedictine convent in Lisieux. They would be day students at this excellent institution. As for me, I was only five. Pauline, my "Little Mother," would be my teacher until I was old enough to go to the convent.

The days at *The Elms* were busy ones. Each morning I had lessons with Pauline. If I did well with these, I was allowed to go for a long walk with Papa in the afternoon. On these walks we always made a visit to the Blessed Sacrament in one of the many churches in Lisieux. One day we entered a chapel not far from our house. In the sanctuary I noticed a large iron grating.

"Look, Little Queen," whispered Papa, "behind that grating holy nuns are praying for sinners."

I leaned forward eagerly but could not see the nuns. Papa then explained that the good Sisters were Carmelites. They were hidden from the world so that they could give all their time to loving God and bringing others to love Him. Only very close relatives could see the Sisters in the parlor, and then just for a short time.

I listened attentively to everything Papa said and told Marie and Pauline about our visit when we returned home. Both were much interested for they had not known that a Carmelite monastery was in the neighborhood.

So the days passed. Sometimes Papa took me fishing, a recreation which he enjoyed a great deal. Back in Alencon he had spent many happy hours angling, and the major part of his catch was always sent to the Poor Clare convent. In Lisieux, fishing was still his favorite pastime, and of course I was delighted to go with him. He bought me a rod and line of my own, and I tried very hard to become expert. But generally I tired of waiting for the fish to bite. I much preferred to sit beside Papa on the quiet river bank and think and dream. Sometimes my thoughts were really prayers. If the country is so beautiful, I reflected, the river and trees, what must Heaven be like?

I enjoyed the daily excursions with Papa after lessons were over, but the favorite day of the week for me was Sunday. How I looked forward to this! There was no work then. In the morning the whole family attended High Mass in the Cathedral, returning in the afternoon for the beautiful service of Compline. Sometimes we spent the evening with Uncle Isidore and Aunt Celine. I always enjoyed these visits. My uncle was a clever man, and I was flattered that he treated me as though I were a much older child. I liked to hear him talk, even though many times the subjects were quite over my head. Once in a while he would also sing for me in his deep bass voice. Whenever the song was his favorite, one about the cruel tyrant Bluebeard, I would look at him with frightened eyes. How he would laugh then! Why was I so fearful? Didn't I know that Bluebeard was only a make-believe person?

One night when Papa was taking me home from the Guerin house, I saw a beautiful sight in the sky. The stars had formed the letter T, very large and plain.

"Look, Papa!" I cried eagerly. "My name is written in Heaven!"

My father laughed. "Little Queen, that isn't your name. That's the constellation Orion."

"It's a T," I said. "Oh, Papa! Take my hand and let me keep on looking at the sky. It's so beautiful!"

So we walked along together, Papa leading me over the rough places while my heart sang with joy. Surely I was born for great things! Even the stars spelled out my initial for everyone to see!

In the days when I lived, it was not customary for boys and girls to make their First Communion at the age of six or seven. No, a child had to wait until the year when his eleventh birthday occurred. But it was possible to make one's First Confession much earlier. Accordingly, this privilege was given to me in 1879, when I was six years old. It was Pauline who took me to church for the big event.

I had been well instructed as to the meaning of Confession. I understood that the priest represents God, that he has the power to forgive sins if one is truly sorry for them. Because of this, I asked my "Little Mother" if I should not tell the priest, Father Ducellier, that I loved him with all my heart.

"No, just tell him your sins," said Pauline. "That will be enough."

I was so small that I had to stand up to make my confession. When it was over, I passed my rosary through the grating and asked Father Ducellier if he would bless it for me. The good priest did so. Presently I went outside to join Pauline. A prayer Mama had taught me came into my mind, and I said it as fervently as I could.

> My God, I give You my heart.
> May it please You to accept it, so that
> no creature can take possession of it
> but You alone, my good Jesus!"

It had grown dark while we were in the church, and on the way home I stopped for a moment under a street light.

"Therese, what are you doing?" asked my big sister curiously.

I stared at her with puzzled eyes. "The rosary looks just as it did before," I said slowly. "Oh, Pauline! I thought the blessing would make a difference!"

My sister laughed. Then she explained that the blessing *had* made a difference, although I could not see it. From now on, the prayers offered on this little string of beads would be more pleasing to God. They would be of great help to the Souls in Purgatory also.

How I admired Pauline! She knew so much and did everything to fill Mama's place where I was concerned. But she would not agree that I ought to be allowed to receive Holy Communion, now that I had been to Confession. When I suggested that maybe I should tell the Bishop how much I wanted this great favor, she shook her head. I was no

"I THOUGHT THE BLESSING WOULD MAKE A DIFFERENCE!"

different from other children. I must wait until 1884, the year when I would be eleven years old.

My love for Pauline was very great, and so I never dreamed of arguing. I continued to bring her my little problems, knowing that she could settle everything. For instance, one day I was worried about the happiness of the blessed in Heaven. I knew that some saints are greater than others, being possessed of more glory. Well, what about the lesser saints? Are they unhappy because of this?

Pauline took my little thimble and a large drinking glass belonging to Papa. She filled both to the brim with water. Then, smiling into my anxious face, she told me to look closely.

"Which is the fuller?" she asked. "The thimble or the glass?"

At once I understood. The little thimble represented one soul, the large glass another. Each could hold no more water than Pauline had put in it. Without any trouble I realized that the example could also be applied to Heaven. Here the saints reflect just that beauty and perfection which God has decided for them. Each is "full", and there can never be any sorrow because some are little thimbles and others large glasses.

There was another good lesson which Pauline taught me. This occurred one day when I returned home from a long walk with Papa. I was very hot and tired and lost no time in saying so.

"If you only knew how thirsty I am!" I told Pauline. "I'm nearly dead for a drink of water!"

My sister smiled. "Don't you want to go without a drink to help some poor sinner?" she asked gently.

I hesitated. After all, I was terribly thirsty. Yet grace triumphed in the end, and with a big sigh I told Pauline that I would make the sacrifice. My sister seemed pleased with this and went off about her work. A few minutes later she came back. In her hand was a cool and refreshing drink.

"This is for you," she told me. "Sit down and enjoy it, dear."

I was almost in tears. I wanted the drink so much, yet what about the unknown sinner I had promised to help? Surely it wouldn't be right to abandon him!

Seeing my distress, Pauline told me not to worry. "You have gained the merit of the sacrifice," she said kindly. "Now you can gain the merit of obedience, too. Ah, my dear, how much that will mean for your sinner!"

CHAPTER 4

A MYSTERIOUS ILLNESS

OCCASIONALLY Papa had to leave *The Elms* because of business affairs. One of these trips occurred when I was six years old. A few days after he left, I was standing alone at a window which overlooked the garden. Suddenly my heart gave a great leap. A man was walking in the garden. And it was Papa!

"Papa! Papa!" I called excitedly, but there was no answer. He did not even turn toward the window, but continued to walk steadily down the path. Suddenly fear seized me. Papa looked so drooped and old! And there was a heavy veil over his head. What did it mean? And why didn't he pay any attention to his Little Queen?

Marie and Pauline were in a nearby room. Hearing my cries, they hurried to see what was wrong.

"Why are you calling Papa when he is in Alencon?" asked Marie anxiously. "Don't you know better than that, Therese?"

Tears were falling down my cheeks as I pointed to the window. "He's come back!" I sobbed. "He walked toward the fir trees and then disappeared!"

Pauline looked at me in amazement. "That couldn't be, child. Papa would never come back without letting us know."

I continued to sob, talking brokenly about the veil over Papa's head. Suddenly Marie hit upon the explanation that the maid, Victoria, had played a trick on me. She had put her apron over her head and then walked past the window, pretending that she was Papa.

"No, no!" I cried. "It really was Papa. I saw him. And he looked so old and sad!"

There was no doubt about it. I was in a bad state of fright. At once my sisters went to the kitchen to question Victoria. Had she played a trick on me? Had she pretended to be Papa? Victoria was indignant. She was too busy for tricks. She had not left the kitchen for hours.

Presently all of us made a thorough search of the garden, but to no avail. Papa was not there. Or any stranger. I must have imagined the whole thing.

"Don't think any more about it," said Marie comfortingly. "Little girls often make mistakes."

Think no more about it? How could I not think of it! Yet I did my best to obey. Perhaps some day the meaning of what I had seen would be clear. In the meantime, my heart was filled with sadness. The veil which had hidden Papa's face from me: did it mean that some dreadful misfortune was in store for him?

Two years later Leonie finished her studies at the Benedictine convent, and it was decided that I should take her place. It was now October, 1881, and I was only a few months short of my ninth birthday. Everyone felt that it was time for me to have other teachers than Pauline. I did not agree with this, for I had no desire to leave my "Little Mother", to go into surroundings where everything was new and different. Because Papa wished it, however, I did not complain and did my best to study hard. God blessed these efforts, and before long I was in a class of girls much older than I. The Benedictine nuns were pleased with such progress, as was the convent chaplain, Father Domin. He began to call me his "Little Doctor", for Pauline had been an excellent teacher and I knew quite a bit about religion.

I was not very happy at school, however. Some of the girls, jealous that a nine-year-old should be in their classes, plagued me and made me miserable. I did not know how to defend myself, nor had I any real wish to do so. In my own simple way, I thought it was God's Will that I suffer their taunts. But I was always cheerful in the late afternoons, knowing that soon it would be time to return to *The Elms.* Indeed, Papa and my older sisters had no idea that I was so unhappy at school. They saw me only when I was smiling, grateful for being with them again in our pretty home. And the fact that I made good marks and was nearly always first in a class of much older girls pleased them very much.

"It's a good thing that we sent Therese to school," said Papa one day. "She's getting along splendidly."

Celine and our little cousins, Jane and Marie Guerin, were quite happy at the Benedictine convent. They were not as sensitive as I and no one bothered to tease them. One day as we walked home together from school, Marie and I decided to play one of our favorite games.

"Hermits are not interested in the world," I told my cousin. "Marie, I'm going to pretend that I'm a really holy hermit. I'll shut my eyes and you can lead me down the street."

Generally Marie liked the games I suggested, but this time she thought her part no fun at all. "Why can't I be a hermit, too?" she asked. "Why do I have to lead you?"

Finally we decided we could both be hermits. We would shut our eyes and only the very holiest thoughts would be ours. So it was done, and for a time all went well. We were really model hermits. Then sudden calamity struck as Marie and I bumped into a display of vegetables outside a grocery store. There was a fearful clatter and thudding as piles of crates tumbled down around us. Instantly our eyes shot open on a terrifying scene. Vegetables were rolling all over the sidewalk, and the grocer, startled at the commotion, was rushing to the door.

"Why don't you look where you're going?" he roared angrily. "Such stupid children!"

We took one look at the damage, at the grocer, then started to run. Only when we had put a safe distance between ourselves and the grocery store did we venture to stop for breath.

"We mustn't play at hermits again!" panted Marie, frightened and dismayed. "It's too dangerous!"

I agreed, sadly. Undoubtedly it was best for hermits to live far away from grocery stores.

A year after I entered the Benedictine convent as a day student, Pauline decided to become a Carmelite nun. For years I had felt that some day she would give herself to God, but now that our separation was at hand my heart almost broke. Pauline, my "Little Mother," was going away! Never again would she be at *The Elms* to greet me after an unhappy day at school!

Seeing my distress, Pauline did her best to comfort me. She described the beauty of the Carmelite life, telling me that she was going away to pray and suffer for souls. Priests would be her particular care. She would offer her life that God might bless the world with many good and holy priests.

My sister's words impressed me deeply, and one night my heart thrilled to a sudden and wonderful knowledge. I, too, was called to be a Carmelite nun! Hurriedly I set out to find Pauline to tell her this glorious thought. Now there was no need for us to be separated. I also would go to the monastery to pray and suffer for souls.

Instead of laughing, Pauline embraced me tenderly. Then, as gently as she could, she explained that little girls of nine cannot be nuns. The laws of the Church will not permit it.

"Later on you will be able to come," she promised.

It was a bitter disappointment that I could not accompany my sister to Carmel. I confessed my wish to the Prioress, Mother Mary Gonzaga, who listened patiently to all my troubles but in the end agreed with Pauline. I could not be a Carmelite at the age of nine. Later on the nuns would see whether or not I had a vocation. If I did, I could enter freely. And I would be given the beautiful name of Sister Therese of the Child Jesus.

I was only partly consoled, and soon school became a real torment. Even *The Elms* lost its charm. My "Little Mother" had become Sister Agnes of Jesus. When I visited her in the convent parlor, there was an iron grating between us. No longer could I claim her as my own.

A few months after Pauline left us, Papa went to Paris. Marie and Leonie accompanied him, while Celine and I continued our school work at the Benedictine convent. Alas! The strain of my big sister's departure for Carmel soon began to tell on me, and during Holy Week I fell ill. Uncle Isidore sent word to Papa that he had better return to Lisieux at once. His Little Queen was in a serious state.

Poor Papa! He had been enjoying his visit in Paris, particularly the opportunity of taking Marie and Leonie to the beautiful Holy Week services. But he promptly left everything to return to my side. There was good reason for this, since in the days that followed I became desperately ill. Sometimes I did not even recognize Papa. I cried out that his hat was a terrible black beast. I turned away from my sisters and even tried to throw myself out of bed!

Sadly the doctor announced that he could do nothing. Even if I did recover, my mind would be affected. Only prayer could help. At this dreadful report, everyone set to work to ask God for my cure. The result was what seemed a great improvement, so that I was allowed out of bed, and when the time came for Pauline to receive the Carmelite habit, I was taken to the ceremony. But the next day I was much worse and had to go to bed again. In despair, Papa wrote to Paris to have a Novena of Masses offered for me at the Shrine of Our Lady of Victories.

On Sunday, during the novena, Marie went out to the garden for a little walk. Leonie was reading near the window in my room. I had been quiet in bed, but suddenly I became greatly excited and began to call for my big sister. Marie rushed back to my side, but it was too late. I could no longer recognize her. I felt alone with the Devil. He was everywhere about, fighting to take my soul from God. I struggled in torment. I tossed about to avoid his clutches. I tried to jump out of bed, to run away, but I could not. All I could do was to moan and tremble in agony.

My sisters were beside themselves with fear. What had happened to their little Therese? Her face was twisted and strange. She no longer knew them. Marie, my second mother, felt that she was failing me. In a burst of grief, she threw herself on her knees at the foot of my bed.

"Don't let Therese die!" she cried, casting an imploring glance at a statue of the Blessed Virgin. "Holy Mother, give her back to us strong and well!"

Leonie and Celine joined their prayers to Marie's. They thought that I was unconscious, but I was praying, too. Despite all appearances, I knew that my dear ones were storming Heaven for my life.

Suddenly, through God's Mercy, I felt a marvelous peace flood my soul. The Devil no longer had power over me! As the glorious release came, I turned my eyes to the statue of the Blessed Virgin. What joy! It was a statue no longer. It was real! Our Lady, beautiful and radiant in her blue robe, was smiling at me! She had heard my sisters' prayers! I was cured!

Marie was the first to sense the change in me. Rising from her knees, she came toward me and gazed long and tenderly into my eyes.

"Do you feel better now, little one?"

I smiled faintly, unable to speak. Deep in my heart I knew that a miracle had taken place.

"But I will tell no one," I thought. "If I do, all my happiness will vanish."

CHAPTER 5

MY FIRST HOLY COMMUNION

MARIE was as certain as I that a great wonder had taken place, and in the end I shared my secret with her. Yes—I was myself again. The Blessed Virgin had smiled upon me and made me well. Overjoyed at the good news, my sister carried the story to Carmel that same day. Very soon it had made the rounds, and when I was taken to see Pauline, the nuns were ready with dozens of questions. Had the Blessed Virgin spoken to me? Had the vision lasted one minute? Two minutes? Five minutes? How was Our Lady dressed? Had the Christ Child been with her? Did she appear young or old?

I tried to answer these and other questions truthfully, but very soon I became worried. What had happened, really? A miracle, of course, but a miracle which did not lend itself to long description. Our Lady had smiled and cured me. That was all.

Seeing that I was reluctant to talk, some of the nuns made light of the whole affair. Others remarked that I was being wicked in not answering their questions more fully. Soon I became confused and tearful, for now the miracle had become a source of scruples. Because of it many people thought I was an obstinate child who delighted in being the center of attraction. How much better if I could have kept Our Lady's smile to myself!

I had been cured on May 13, 1883, at the age of ten years and four months. The following spring Marie undertook to prepare me for my First Communion. I listened eagerly to her instructions and asked if I might spend half an hour a day "in meditation", a practice of which I had heard at school and which I felt I should learn.

Marie refused, for she was still fearful of my health. Then I begged permission to spend fifteen minutes in daily meditation. Again I was refused. Regretfully I stopped asking for the great favor, but on half-holidays from school I would go to my room, sit down on the bed and pull the curtains about me. Hidden in this way I thought about God, the shortness of life, the mystery of eternity. Marie soon suspected what I was doing, but I was not scolded. She knew it was quite by accident that I had stumbled on the real meaning of meditation.

The day chosen for my First Communion was May 8. The week preceding I spent at the convent with other girls who were to receive Our Lord for the first time. It was really a retreat, during which we prayed and thought about the wonderful privilege that soon would be ours. Father Domin and the Benedictine nuns continued our instructions, and though I had never been away from home by myself before, I was not lonely. The thought that soon Our Lord would come to me was enough to banish any sadness.

Finally the great day came, and it is impossible to describe what took place in my heart. In all my eleven years I had never been so happy. I was so filled with joy at the time of Communion that I cried. At this some of the other girls began to whisper among themselves.

"Therese has remembered a big sin," said one of them.

"No, she is crying because her mother is dead," put in another.

"She misses Pauline," added a third.

None of these things was true. I cried because I was feeling the greatest joy a person can know in this life: the joy of having God within one's heart! Apparently none of my little friends understood, for afterwards they looked at me curiously. Not one of them had shed a tear, and they could see no reason for my crying either.

When Our Lord came into my heart for the first time, I felt He loved me very much. In return I

"THERESE HAS REMEMBERED A BIG SIN!"

said that I also loved Him. Then I asked Him to take away my liberty and do with me as He pleased. Now I was truly like the raindrop which loses itself in the vast ocean, for by this request I had lost myself in the greatness of God. We were united forever! After all, who can separate a raindrop from the ocean?

That afternoon, in the name of my companions, I recited the Act of Consecration to the Blessed Virgin in the convent chapel. Later Papa took me to the Carmelite monastery for a visit with Pauline. By a strange coincidence it was her Profession Day—the day when she had made a solemn promise to belong to God forever. Now she was wearing a wreath of roses on her head, a sign of the reward that some day would be hers for having served God faithfully in her cloister home.

How happy I was to see my "Little Mother", to tell her of my First Communion at the convent! As we talked, the big iron grating seemed to disappear, and our souls were united in a common joy. After this there was even more happiness, for that night I was the guest of honor at a fine dinner. All my dear ones were present, and each brought a gift in remembrance of my First Communion. Of these, Papa's was by far the nicest—a beautiful watch.

Amid all the celebration, I realized very clearly that a person cannot stand still on the long journey to Heaven. Each day he either goes forward or backward, becomes more or less holy. And it is all a matter of personal choice!

"I don't want to go backward," I thought. "I want to be a saint. I want to use all the grace God has in store for me."

Long ago I had learned in my Catechism that grace is the coin with which human beings can purchase Heaven. Grace gives strength. God is most generous with it, and this despite the fact that millions of people never bother to notice His kindness. Before going to bed, I took my notebook and wrote down three resolutions which I felt would bring me extra grace. The resolutions were these:

1. I will never give way to discouragement.
2. I will say the *Memorare* every day.
3. I will try to humble my pride.

Five weeks later, after another retreat at the convent, I received the Sacrament of Confirmation. The Holy Spirit came into my heart with His seven great gifts: Wisdom, understanding, counsel, fortitude, knowledge, piety and fear of the Lord. I had need of all these gifts, especially of fortitude, for by now the joy of my First Communion Day had disappeared. I was fearful of everything. I saw sin in even the simplest pleasures. I felt I was no longer a friend of God. I was one more of the wicked people in the world who turn away from His grace.

I brought all these troubles to Marie, who knew how to give good advice. Over and over again she comforted me, saying that I was really God's friend; that He still lived in my heart; that He was only putting my love to a test. I believed her and tried to be at peace, but in a few hours fresh scruples would come. Then the tears would stream down my cheeks and my head would start to ache. What a dreadful thing to be a sinner! To be kept away forever from the joys of Heaven!

As a result of endless worry about the state of my soul, my health began to suffer. The following spring I was twelve years old, and Aunt Celine decided a vacation at the seashore was what I needed. She rented a house and took her two daughters, Jane and Marie, as companions for me.

At first all went well. I enjoyed catching shrimps, riding a donkey down the sandy beach, climbing among the rocks in search of pretty stones and shells. The sight of the ocean also thrilled me. It was so beautiful in fine weather, so full of wonder in a storm! To all appearances I was fast regaining my strength amid the healthful surroundings which Aunt Celine had chosen. Then one day I startled everybody by bursting into tears.

"What's the trouble now?" asked Aunt Celine. "Another scruple?"

I nodded, ashamed of being such a nuisance, but convinced I must tell someone of my latest fault. That morning I had tied my hair with a blue ribbon. The effect of the blue against my fair curls had given me pleasure. I had admired myself in the mirror.

"But that wasn't a sin!" cried my aunt. "All

girls your age wear ribbons in their hair. Don't be so stupid, child!"

In my heart I felt Aunt Celine was right, but I could not be at peace until I had told this "sin" in Confession. Even then I was worried. Had I forgotten some other sin? Was I really in the state of grace? Was God pleased with me?

I returned to school in the fall, alone this time, for by now Celine had finished her studies. I worked hard and the nuns seemed pleased with my efforts but at Christmas Papa decided I was not strong enough to be away from home all day. The scruples that had been tormenting me for so many months were more insistent than ever. I suffered from constant headaches. I was nervous beyond description and cried at the least thing. It would be better for me to have a tutor.

So, after my thirteenth birthday, I had private lessons with a woman teacher in Lisieux. Frequently visitors came to see this lady's mother and sometimes I heard them whispering at the other end of the large room where I was studying.

"Who is that pretty little girl?" asked one.

"What lovely golden curls!" declared another.

My teacher's mother agreed with everything that was said. Yes, I was a pretty child. And an excellent student. What a pity that my health was so poor!

I tried to be very busy with my lessons, but all these flattering remarks reached my ears. The result was that first I was excited with pleasure, then distressed. What about the third resolution I had made after receiving my First Communion? Since that happy day I really had done very little about humbling my pride. Indeed, no one would dream I was a girl who longed to be a Carmelite nun. How fretful I was! How easily I cried!

Some months later I decided to make a real effort to overcome these childish traits. One of the new resolutions was to be enrolled as a Child of Mary. I felt Our Lady would be pleased at this proof of my devotion, particularly as it meant returning to school, where I had never been very happy or made close friends.

To everyone's surprise, I began going to the Benedictine convent two or three times a week. With other future members of the Sodality, I passed this time in sewing and in listening to religious instruction. When the time came for recreation, however, I escaped to the chapel. I felt that the other girls knew there was something peculiar about me, and I could not bear to be questioned or teased. Far from being overcome, my pride was as great as on that day when I had refused to kiss the ground for Mama's penny!

The acceptance as a Child of Mary on May 31, 1886, marked the end of my connection with the Benedictine convent. But it did not end my scruples. I was still timid and fearful, and when Marie announced that she would be leaving for Carmel in October, I was beside myself with grief. First

Mama, then Pauline, now Marie! At the age of thirteen I had already lost three mothers!

I tried very hard to be brave. After all, there was no need for me to be a baby all my life.

"I will pray to those little ones who died before I was born," I thought. "Surely *they* will help me."

Marie Helen, Marie Melanie, Joseph Louis, John Baptist—how earnestly I asked these little sisters and brothers for strength and courage!

"Give me peace!" I begged. "Let me feel that you little ones in Heaven still know how to love poor Therese!"

This prayer was wonderfully answered. Almost immediately a great calm entered my soul. Gone were the scruples, the foolish doubts that had plagued me for years. Once again I felt that God was really living within me, that I was as united to Him as the raindrop which loses itself in the great ocean.

This gift did not disappear but grew even more pronounced as time passed. Yet there was another gift which I desired with all my heart. This was the loss of my extreme self-consciousness. I was so easily hurt! I cried over the least little disappointment. Afterwards I cried because I had cried.

"Dear Lord, help me to grow up!" I prayed. "Work a miracle, if necessary, but somehow make me brave!"

Marie had left us on October 15 for the Carmelite monastery. A few weeks later, Our Lord worked the miracle I had desired so much. Early on

Christmas morning, after I had received Him in Holy Communion at Midnight Mass, I realized many things which I had never thought of before. I saw God as a little child, seemingly weak, yet holding in His hands the power to rule the universe. He had taken to Himself human flesh and blood, thereby elevating the whole human race so that it shared in His strength. In an instant He let me see that I was meant to use my share of that strength, not to doubt it. By myself I was a creature of tears and sighs and complaints, but with Christ as a Brother I possessed courage beyond my fondest dreams.

CHAPTER 6

MY FIRST CHILD OF GRACE

HOW HAPPY I was as I walked home from Midnight Mass with Papa and my sisters! The strength of soul which had left me at Mama's death was back again. The shyness and tears had gone the way of foolish scruples. I was a new person.

There was a good chance to prove this when we reached the house. Following the Christmas Eve custom of little French children, I had left my shoes by the fireplace some hours earlier, knowing that Papa and my sisters would fill them with presents. Now, as Celine and I started upstairs to take off our things, we heard our good father say that I was too big for such childishness. He hoped it would be the last time I expected my shoes to be filled with gifts.

Ordinarily, I should have been grief-stricken at hearing Papa speak this way. Now everything was different. There was no need for Celine to hover anxiously about me, ready to dry my tears. I was brave at last. God had worked a miracle during my Christmas Communion. I was now strong with His strength, and to Celine's amazement I went downstairs in a few minutes and took the presents from my shoes with every sign of joy. Truly, Christmas Day of 1886 was the beginning of my conversion. Never again was I to be entirely the victim of childish tears.

A short time later God gave me another great grace. One Sunday as I closed my prayerbook at the end of Mass, a picture of the Crucifixion slipped out from the pages, showing one of the Saviour's pierced hands. At the sight of the Precious Blood falling to earth, I was struck with an intense desire to stand in spirit at the foot of the Cross to receive this Blood and pour It out upon sinners. I longed to suffer for souls as Christ had done, so that some day they might be happy with Him forever. The desire for the life of a Carmelite increased, too — for that life which is made up of hidden prayer and sacrifice. Now more than ever did it seem to me a thing of beauty, and I longed with all my heart to embrace it.

I said nothing to Papa, however. He was not too well these days, and something told me that it was not wise to leave him. Instead, God would let me save souls while I stayed at home. He would inspire me to devote myself to those about me, to be kind and cheerful and willing. Such actions were not too hard for a girl of fourteen, yet how valuable they could be if I offered them to the Heavenly Father in union with the sufferings of Jesus Christ.

My first duties in this new life of charity were towards my own family. I tried very hard to be useful about the house, and my sisters soon noted the change which had come over me. I tried to be kind to our servants and to the poor who came each Monday to the back door for food. When the opportunity arose to teach Catechism to two little girls, I seized it eagerly. How I loved children! They seemed to love me, too, and many were the happy hours I spent with these little friends, telling them of the good God and the wonderful reward He has prepared for those who serve Him faithfully.

To all appearances I was just a normal girl, living quietly with her family. I did nothing out of the ordinary. There were no miracles or visions, only days of prayer and little works of mercy. But people would have been very much surprised if they could have read my heart. I was on fire with a desire to save souls! I thirsted for them!

Because of this, I sometimes wondered if I should not join a missionary Order instead of the cloistered Carmelites. With God's grace, I might do wonderful things for souls in China, in Africa, in distant islands. I might teach Catechism to little pagan children. I might nurse the sick and comfort the dying. But the thought always persisted that more souls can be saved by sacrifice than by any other means. God seemed to whisper in my heart that I was meant to lead a life of prayer and penance rather than to work as a missionary in foreign lands.

I was delighted when Celine told me that she shared my desire to be a Carmelite. Already our sister Leonie was making plans to enter the Poor Clares. This meant that some day the five living children of our family would be consecrated to God's service.

"But what about Papa?" I asked suddenly. "Is it right for us to leave him all alone?"

Celine was kindness itself. "Don't worry," she said. "You may go to Carmel first. I will stay with Papa as long as he lives."

I marveled at my sister's generosity. She was nearly four years older than I, but she was willing to allow me to go first into the Lord's service. What wonderful charity! Surely God would bless her a hundredfold.

Speaking of my vocation to Papa was a real problem. The weeks passed, and still I could not bring myself to do it. Already he had been very generous, permitting Pauline and Marie to leave for Carmel and Leonie for the Poor Clares. But what would he say at losing another daughter?

"Maybe the Feast of Pentecost would be a good time to tell him," I thought. "Dear God, let me be very strong on that day!"

The family assisted at all the church services on Pentecost. After Vespers, Papa was a little tired and went out to the garden to rest. I watched him, knowing that now the time had come. It was sunset. Birds were singing in the tall trees. The whole world was at peace. In the beautiful surroundings of our garden, I would tell my good father that God had chosen me for His own.

When I went outside to the place where he was sitting, I was cold and trembling, and my eyes were full of tears.

"Could I talk with you a little while, Papa?"

Seeing that I was troubled about something, my father got to his feet and put an arm about me. Very slowly we began to walk down the path.

"What is it, Little Queen?" he asked. "Tell me."

I laid my head against his heart. "I want to be a Carmelite," I whispered. "I want to join Marie and Pauline at Christmas."

Poor Papa! How his heart was torn at these words! He had expected to hear them some day, but not while I was so young—only fourteen. For a moment he could not speak. Then he recovered himself and led me still farther down the garden. Presently we stopped beside some little white lilies. Papa bent down and picked one of them for me.

"This flower is like your heart, child," he said gently. "White and pure. I won't stand in your way if you wish to give it to God."

Now happiness was mixed with my tears. Papa had given his consent! I might enter Carmel on

Christmas Day, the first anniversary of that happy occasion when the Christ Child had made me strong with His own strength! Everything was settled at last.

But things were far from being settled. First, Uncle Isidore was really angry. What was the matter with Papa that he was willing to let a mere child enter a cloistered Order?

"It's ridiculous!" he fumed. "I'll do everything I can to stop such nonsense!"

Marie was also against my cherished dream. Unlike Pauline, she thought I should wait until I was twenty-one before entering Carmel. Then there was Canon Delatroette, the priest who watched over the affairs of the community. He refused to allow the Prioress to receive me into the cloister.

"Never!" he cried. "To hear you talk, one would think the salvation of the community depended upon this child. Let her wait until she has come of age."

I was dreadfully disappointed. In my heart I knew God wished me to be a Carmelite. Then why were there so many obstacles? Such criticism and misunderstanding?

"Don't worry," said Papa after an unhappy interview with Canon Delatroette. "You and I will go to the Bishop of Bayeux and state our case. He has the power to grant your desire."

I began to feel better. "Can we go soon?" I asked.

Papa laughed. "Not for several weeks, Little Queen. The Bishop is an important man, you know. We'll have to write for an appointment."

After some days, a reply came from the Vicar General, Father Révérony. The Bishop of Bayeux would see Papa and me on October 31.

How far away this seemed, for it was now only June. What should I do with myself in the meantime?

"*Pray for sinners,*" said a little voice in my heart. "*Look about and do good.*"

At this time the greatest sinner I could imagine was a man named Pranzini. During the last few days, the papers had made constant mention of him. Some said no worse criminal had lived in France than this unfortunate man. Not only had he tortured and murdered two defenseless women and a little child, but he now refused to show any remorse for what he had done. He boasted and blasphemed. No priest could do anything for him.

My heart ached at the thought of what lay in store for Pranzini. The court had sentenced him to be executed in September. If he did not repent before then, he would surely go to Hell.

"I must help him," I told myself. "Dear God, please let me have this poor man's soul!"

I had often prayed for people before, for special favors and graces, but this was the first time I had ever set myself to praying for a really bad person. Knowing that human actions have enormous value when offered to God by His Son, I consecrated all my efforts and asked Christ to present them to the Heavenly Father for my intention. I also called upon the saints and angels for help.

Day and night I prayed for Pranzini, consoled by the thought that I was doing the work of a Carmelite while still in the world, that my prayers and sacrifices could really be offered to save a soul for Heaven. But great as was my confidence that God would hear me, my heart cried out for a visible sign. After all, Pranzini was my first sinner. Was it asking too much to have evidence of his conversion?

"Let me know when he returns to You," I begged God. *"Please!"*

Weeks passed, and presently it was the end of August. Pranzini had showed no sign of repentance. The newspapers continued to tell of his wickedness, his refusal to go to Confession, the dreadful things he said against religion. Still I did not give up hope. Pranzini was "my first child." I simply would not let him go to Hell.

The day after the execution I could not wait to look at the paper. Surely my sinner had returned to God, but what if I was never to know for sure! With thudding heart I began to read the account of his last moments. Suddenly I stopped. *"Just before he died, Pranzini asked for the chaplain's crucifix! He kissed it three times!"*

Gratitude swept into my heart, and I could read no more. My sinner, my first child, was saved!

Two months later came the day I had longed for, yet dreaded — October 31, when Papa and I were to have our interview with the Bishop of Bayeux. The desire to look older than my fourteen years was so great that for the first time in my life I did up my long curls. As I observed the effect in a mirror, I felt very dignified. No one could call me a child now. I was a real young lady, one who knew what she wanted. The Bishop would observe this and grant my desire to enter Carmel on Christmas Day.

Alas! My heart sank lower with every step of the journey, and when Papa and I arrived at the Bishop's house, I felt miserably young. The Vicar General, Father Révérony, met us at the door. Seeing tears in my eyes, he gave me a reassuring smile.

"You must not let His Lordship see those diamonds," he said.

We passed from one enormous room to another, and I began to feel like a tiny ant. What was I going to say to the Bishop? And how dreadful if I cried! Even as I prayed for help, we came to a room where three large armchairs were arranged before a glowing fire. As the Bishop entered, Papa and I knelt for his blessing. Then we were told to be seated. Father Révérony indicated that the chair in the middle was for me.

"No, thank you, Father," I said timidly, for the Bishop and Papa had taken the side chairs, and there seemed no place for the Vicar General.

"Let us see how obedient you are," said the latter kindly. At this I slipped into the middle chair without a word. How lost I felt! The chair was big enough to hold four girls my size!

For a moment all was quiet. I hoped Papa would speak first, but he motioned for me to begin. With a shy glance at the Bishop, and at Father Révérony who had chosen an ordinary chair for himself, I started to explain the reason for our visit. On January 2 I would be fifteen years old. I wished to enter the Carmelite monastery in Lisieux on Christmas Day. Most people thought I was too young, but if His Lordship would give the word. . . .

The Bishop leaned toward me, a little smile on his face. "You have wanted to be a Carmelite for a long time, child?"

I nodded eagerly. "A very long time, Your Lordship."

"But certainly not as long as fifteen years," put in Father Révérony.

"No, Father. But since the age of three I have wanted to give myself to the good God."

The Bishop felt that Papa might be sad because I wanted to leave him. He suggested, gently, that perhaps I had better stay at home a little longer. The three sisters who were already nuns could attend to the prayers. I would be pleasing God in other ways.

At this my father shook his head. "Your Lordship, I am as eager as Therese that you grant her request," he said. "And if you cannot help her, we shall go to Rome and speak to the Holy Father. There is a pilgrimage leaving Paris in a few days. We plan to make it."

The Bishop was much impressed. Not often did he meet with such a generous parent. However, he said that it would be impossible for him to do anything about my vocation without first speaking to Canon Delatroette, the superior of the Carmelites in Lisieux.

Fresh tears glistened in my eyes. I clasped my hands fervently and turned an imploring glance upon the Bishop. "But we have already spoken to him, Your Lordship, and he thinks I'm only a baby. Oh, he will never do anything to help!"

The next minute I had forgotten my resolution to act like a grown-up person. I was crying as though my heart would break. Papa and Father Révérony looked silently at each other as the Bishop tried to comfort me.

"There, there," he said kindly. "All is not lost, little one. And I am very pleased about the pilgrimage to Rome. You will have a really wonderful time with your good father. Now, how would you like to come with me for a look at our garden?"

I rose to my feet blindly. What did I care about a garden? The trip to Bayeux had been a failure. The Bishop thought I was a child. He would never allow me to enter Carmel on Christmas Day.

CHAPTER 7

DISAPPOINTMENT IN ROME

E were heavy-hearted on the trip home, although Papa did his best to comfort me with exciting descriptions of the many wonderful sights we should see on our pilgrimage to Rome.

"Then we're really going, Papa?"

"Yes, child. And don't look so sad. The Bishop didn't give his consent for you to enter Carmel at Christmas, but it may be a different story when we talk to the Holy Father."

These words made me feel much better. Four days later, when Papa, Celine and I set out for Paris, I was really happy. This was my first visit to the greatest city in France, and I was very excited at the prospect of spending three days here. There were so many things to see! So much to do!

But as it turned out the museums, the monuments, the shops, the beautiful avenues and parks, were not what impressed me most. No, it was the little church of Our Lady of Victories. Here Papa had had a Novena of Masses offered for me when I was so ill some years before. Here countless wonders had been worked by the Queen of Heaven for those who confidently asked her aid. Well, now that I had the chance, I would ask for a little favor, too. I would ask Our Lady to set my mind at rest on one score: *Had she really smiled on me and cured me when I was ten years old?*

This prayer was answered very quickly. As I knelt before her statue in the church of Our Lady of Victories, the Blessed Virgin let me understand the truth. The "miracle" of May 13, 1883, hadn't been just imagination on my part, as some of the nuns at Carmel had feared. Our Lady really had restored my health. I had not been mistaken about the beautiful smile I had seen on the face of the statue near my bed.

On November 7, Papa, Celine and I gathered with the other pilgrims in the Basilica of the Sacred Heart. We made the Act of Consecration, then proceeded to the train. Celine was as excited as I, and in the days that followed we were constantly exclaiming at the many splendors about us. Never had we seen such beautiful scenery as that of Switzerland, with its mountains and lakes and picturesque cities and towns. I drank in all I could, telling myself that when I was a Carmelite, with only a poor little cell and a patch of sky for scenery, I would remember the lakes, the wonderful mountains and forests through which we were now passing.

"But I'll remember that Heaven is even more beautiful," I thought. "More beautiful than anyone can imagine!"

We stopped in Lucerne, Como, Milan, Venice, Padua and Bologna—visiting churches and shrines, and seeing all the places of historical interest. It was a wonderful privilege to stay a little while in Loreto, where the house in which the Holy Family once lived is preserved. Celine and I received Holy Communion in the Basilica which now encloses this holy house, and were able to touch our rosaries to the wooden bowl which tradition says was used by the Christ Child. But even this wonderful event was only a preparation for the real climax to our travels. In a few hours we were to feast our eyes on Rome, then speak to the Holy Father, the Vicar of Christ on earth!

"God has been very good to us," said Celine, as the train rattled through one Italian village after another. "Therese, we can never thank Him enough for letting Papa bring us with him on this trip."

I agreed. Marie, Pauline and Leonie would have enjoyed this wonderful adventure, too, if only it could have been arranged before their entrance into the cloister.

"I know God has been good," I said. "Certainly we never did anything to deserve *this*."

A few hours later we arrived in the Eternal City. It was night, and we went at once to our hotel. But the next day we were up early to assist at Mass and to see everything of interest. One of the first places we visited was the Coliseum, once the site of games and entertainments for the pagans of ancient Rome.

"Thousands of martyrs died here," whispered Celine in an awed voice. "They were beheaded, and many were torn to bits by wild beasts. Therese, don't you think we ought to kiss the ground?"

I agreed. But suddenly both of us remembered that centuries had passed since the days of the martyrs. The earth that had been soaked by their blood was far below the present surface.

"There's been some digging over there," observed my sister, pointing to a roped-off section in the distance. "Shall we go?"

No sooner said than done. To the amazement of everyone in our group, particularly Papa, Celine and I ran across the Coliseum to the place of the excavations. When we arrived at the gaping hole and saw the great piles of earth and loose stones, we were a little worried. How could we make our way down without assistance? But our desire to kiss the soil of martyrdom was greater than any fear. Heedless of the warnings shouted to us by Papa and the guide, we crawled under the barricade and then began to slip and slide down the dark opening. With amazing success we went down the steep sides of the hole. Suddenly, a few yards away, we glimpsed a flat stone. It was marked with a cross.

"Remember what the guide said?" cried Celine. "That stone is resting on the very place of a martyrdom, Therese. Hurry up!"

Presently the two of us had reached the little marker. Reverently we kissed it, thrilled at the knowledge that we were kneeling on the very spot where brave souls had gone to God so many centuries before. Then, in that dim light, so far below the soil of modern Rome, I offered a little prayer.

"Dear Lord, let me be a martyr, too!" I begged. "*Please!*"

The little adventure did not take long. In a very few minutes, Celine and I had scrambled back up the steep sides of the opening. We were dusty and a bit breathless. Both of us carried a few small stones, souvenirs of our visit, and when Papa saw how pleased we were to have touched the blood-soaked ground of the martyrs, he could not scold us. In fact, he was just a little proud of our courage.

Later that day we visited other holy places, including the Catacombs. Here Celine and I had the rare privilege of lying on a slab of stone where once the body of Saint Cecilia had rested. Before this I had not been particularly interested in Saint Cecilia, the patroness of musicians, but now I felt that she was one of my real friends. It seemed as if the gentle little saint put her hand in mine, that she spoke to me consolingly of God's Mercy. I was doing right to abandon myself to Him, she

"LET ME BE A MARTYR, TOO!" I BEGGED.

said. He was the kindest of Fathers, and would never forget His little daughter. Later I experienced this same feeling after visiting the tomb of Saint Agnes.

Still another great joy was in store for me. After a round of sightseeing, our party finally arrived at the Basilica of the Holy Cross of Jerusalem. Here we venerated several fragments of the True Cross, two of the thorns, and one of the sacred nails. As the religious who had charge of these precious relics was about to put them away, I asked if I might touch one of them.

"Why not?" he said kindly, although there was a little smile on his face that seemed to mean he doubted I could do so.

I looked at the reliquary, then at my hand. There was a tiny opening in the casing through which I thought I could put my little finger. To the surprise of the religious, I succeeded very easily. Yes—I had the wonderful privilege of actually touching one of the sacred nails once bathed in Our Saviour's Blood!

Our audience with the Holy Father had been set for November 20. On the morning of the great day, Celine and I looked out of the hotel window to find that it was raining. Immediately I felt my heart sink. Since babyhood I had always noticed that nice things happened to me in fine weather, with sorrow coming when nature was in a stormy mood. Now I felt that bad news must surely be in store for me. Because it was raining, the Holy Father was not going to grant my great wish of entering Carmel on Christmas Day!

"You mustn't think such things," said Celine firmly. "You must have faith, Therese."

I agreed it was foolish to believe that the weather has anything to do with future events, and so I tried very hard to be cheerful. In a little while I was ready for the day's great adventure, in a black velvet dress with a lace veil over my head. When Papa met us a few minutes later, he laughed at my solemn face.

"Don't be frightened, Little Queen. Everything's going to turn out well."

It was just half-past seven when we reached the Vatican. At once we were ushered into a large room hung with red silk draperies. At one end was an altar, where the Holy Father would offer Mass for us in a little while. As I reflected upon this, and also upon the fact that later I was to kneel at his feet and kiss his ring, my spirits began to rise. Papa had been right. In spite of the rain, now coming down in torrents, this was really a wonderful day.

Promptly at eight o'clock the Holy Father entered the hall and gave his blessing to the waiting crowd. He was dressed in white, with a scarlet mantle about his shoulders. All was hushed and solemn as he knelt for a moment before the altar, then slowly made ready to offer the Holy Sacrifice. Celine and I scarcely dared to breathe. We were actually looking upon Pope Leo the Thirteenth, successor to Saint Peter and the spiritual father of millions of Catholics!

It was with real devotion that Pope Leo offered the Sacrifice of the Mass. Every action proclaimed his deep piety, his genuine faith. Now the recent days of sightseeing, when there had been so few chances to pray, were entirely forgotten. We were gathered together as one family to offer to God the Father the greatest action on earth—the Sacrifice of His Son. And our leader was none other than the Pope, the Bishop of Rome!

After a second Mass, offered by one of the chaplains, we went to the Audience Chamber. Here the pilgrims were to be presented to the Holy Father, who was now seated in an armchair at one end of the room. Celine and I watched in awed silence as the ceremony began. Each pilgrim was being introduced while kneeling at the Holy Father's feet. Here he received the Papal Blessing, a few words of greeting and a medal.

Suddenly my heart sank as I saw a familiar figure fixing me with a stern eye. It was Father Révérony, the Vicar General of Bayeux, who had been present when Papa and I had paid our recent visit to the Bishop. His glance seemed to pierce my very soul, and I realized the reason only too well. Father Révérony, who was to introduce our group, felt sure that I was going to speak to the Holy Father about entering Carmel. And he was determined not to allow it. A mere child was not to bother Pope Leo the Thirteenth with a matter which other superiors could decide.

"Let no one here presume to speak to His Holiness!" he commanded suddenly, his eyes still upon me. In desperation I turned to Celine. Had we made our trip to Rome for nothing? Couldn't I say *one* word to the Holy Father about being a Carmelite?

Celine smiled at my anxious face. "Speak!" she said gently.

Soon it was the turn of our group to be presented. My heart was pounding wildly, my hands were like ice, and I dared not look at Father Révérony. As the long line of pilgrims made its way toward the Pope, Celine smiled again. She did not speak this time, but I understood everything she was thinking. Now that the great moment had arrived, I must not be afraid.

As my turn came, I knelt down quickly, kissed the Pope's foot, then grasped his hand. My eyes were full of tears as I looked into his kindly face.

"Most Holy Father, I have a great favor to ask!"

Father Révérony made an impatient gesture, but Pope Leo the Thirteenth did not seem to notice. He bent toward me, his dark eyes looking deep into mine.

"Most Holy Father, in honor of your Jubilee, will you permit me to enter Carmel at fifteen?"

There! The fateful words were out at last! Trembling, I waited for the verdict. But before

His Holiness could speak, Father Révérony drew himself up stiffly.

"Most Holy Father, this is a child who desires the life of Carmel, but the superiors are at the moment considering the question."

The Pope smiled. "Well, my child, do whatever the superiors decide."

The words were kind, but they were not the ones I wanted to hear. Heedless of rules, of previous instructions, I joined my hands and placed them on the Pope's knees. Then, with all the fervor I could command, I tried again.

"Oh, Holy Father, if only you said 'yes,' everyone else would agree!"

For a long moment Pope Leo the Thirteenth gazed at me earnestly. Finally he spoke:

"Well, my child, you shall enter if it be God's Will."

The other pilgrims were amazed at my actions. Who was this girl who dared to speak to the Holy Father? To place her hands upon his knees? Father Révérony shared in the general dismay, and made a curt motion for me to give place to those behind me. I refused to move, and was just on the point of renewing my petition when two of the Noble Guard ordered me to rise. Seeing that I made no effort to obey, that the tears were streaming down my face and I continued to kneel with my hands on the Holy Father's knees, they came toward me and tried to lift me to my feet. But I would not budge, and finally Father Révérony had to come to their aid. Still weeping, I was led away from the Audience Chamber.

"*Dear God!*" I thought. "*What am I going to do now?*"

CHAPTER 8

CARMEL AT LAST!

LATER in the day I felt a little quieter, for by now I had remembered something very important. A short time before our audience with the Holy Father, I had abandoned myself to the Will of God in a new way. I had told Our Lord that He was to think of me as a little toy, a ball, with which He could play whenever He wished. If He held me to His Heart, well and good. I would glory in it. But if He threw me to the floor, left me in a corner, even pierced me through and through, I would not complain. I was His very own, and existed only to serve Him and to give Him pleasure.

"I am Our Lord's plaything until I die," I told myself. "I must never forget it."

Our pilgrimage was drawing to a close. After

visits to Naples and Pompeii, we set out for the north of Italy, where we stopped briefly at Assisi, Florence, Pisa and Genoa. Then came the return to France. This time our route lay along the Mediterranean, past pretty little villages, through plains covered with orange trees, olives and graceful palms. After stops at Marseilles and Lyons, we finally arrived in Paris. The pilgrimage was over at last.

"Would you like to go on another trip?" Papa asked me, as the train speeded us toward Lisieux and home. "This one could be to the Holy Land, Therese. You would have a wonderful time."

I smiled, then shook my head. Papa was a born traveler. He loved seeing strange places, meeting new friends. As for me, all I desired was to be a Carmelite. I wanted to begin my life's work of saving souls through prayer and sacrifice. And although there seemed no chance that I could do this right away, I still had hopes. Perhaps the Bishop had changed his mind during our month's absence from Lisieux. Perhaps a letter would be waiting for me when I reached home, giving me permission to enter Carmel on Christmas Day.

Alas! There was no letter from the Bishop when we arrived at *The Elms*. A hurried visit to Carmel, where I spoke with Marie, Pauline and Mother Mary Gonzaga, the Prioress, gave me little encouragement. No girl my age had ever entered the Carmel of Lisieux. Apparently no girl my age ever would.

"Don't be discouraged," said Pauline kindly. "Everything is going to be all right."

I nodded, grateful that my "Little Mother" understood how I was suffering. It was not for nothing that I had offered myself to Our Lord to be His plaything. He had taken me at my word, and for the time being had dropped me in the corner.

Then four weeks later, when all hope seemed lost, my release came. On January 1, 1888, the day before my fifteenth birthday, Mother Mary Gonzaga sent word that the Bishop now authorized her to receive me as a postulant. I thought my heart would burst with joy, and tears blinded me as I read her letter. I wanted to fly to the monastery at once, but more patience was to be required of me. Mother Mary Gonzaga did not wish me to come to Carmel until after Lent. She did not think a girl of fifteen should enter the cloister in this season of extra hardship and more intense prayer.

"And she's right!" declared Celine emphatically, seeing how my heart sank. "You know she is, Therese!"

I hid my disappointment as well as I could, although April 9, the date set for my entrance seemed very far away. How could I settle down to life in the world when every part of me ached for the prayerful silence of the cloister? Papa understood, and so did Celine, and both did all they could to make my last weeks at home happy ones. Leonie was a little worried, however. Some months before she had left us to become a Poor Clare, but the life had been too hard, and now she was home again.

"You want to pray a good deal about your vocation," she told me. "Life in the cloister demands more sacrifice than you think, Therese. I know this from experience."

I understood Leonie's anxiety, and I assured her that every day I was praying for grace and strength to be a good religious. I was not entering Carmel merely to escape the trials and temptations of life in the world, least of all to enjoy companionship with Marie and Pauline. I really wanted to save souls. I really wanted to give my life, in union with Christ, for the redemption of sinners.

Slowly the weeks passed. I spent a great deal of time with Papa, for my heart ached at the thought of parting with him. He was almost sixty-five years old, and not too well. It would be a great grief for me to leave him in April, a great sacrifice for him to give me up. Somehow he seemed to read my thoughts. He did everything to comfort me. One day, on his return from a walk in the country, he brought me an unusual present. It was a tiny white lamb, just one day old. Celine and I were delighted with the little creature, and we showered it with attentions. But it died that very day. I was deeply touched, sensing that the lamb's death had a real lesson for me. Some days later I wrote to Marie:

> "We should not become attached to anything on this earth, not even to

things most innocent, for they fail us at the moment we least think. Only the eternal can fully content us."

On the evening of April 8, there was a farewell dinner at *The Elms*. Papa, Celine and Leonie were present, as well as Uncle Isidore, Aunt Celine and our two cousins, Jane and Marie. Everyone was very solemn, which disturbed me not a little. Why should my dear ones be sad, I asked myself, when I am doing the very wonderful thing of giving myself to God?

The same mood prevailed the next morning, when we assisted at Mass in the public chapel of the Carmelite monastery and received Holy Communion. There were tears and sobs on all sides. Even Papa could not control his emotion. The only one who remained calm was I, who so often had given myself to crying. Yet I was troubled, too, now that the moment for my great adventure actually had come. As I walked toward the door of the cloister, my heart beat so violently that I wondered if I was going to die. What agony to say good-bye to Papa, to Celine and Leonie, to my other relatives and friends!

Presently the cloister door opened. I embraced my dear ones once more, then knelt for Papa's blessing. Still weeping, he knelt beside me and raised his hand in the Sign of the Cross. Then I arose and walked across the threshold to where Marie and Pauline, now Sister Mary of the Sacred Heart and Sister Agnes of Jesus, respectively, were waiting to greet me. My heart was filled to overflowing. I was in Carmel at last!

Almost at that very moment I felt the gaze of one person who still looked upon my entrance with disapproval — Canon Delatroette. As the cloister door stood open, he surveyed the little group of nuns gathered about me.

"Well, my Reverend Mothers, you can now chant a *Te Deum*," he announced grimly. "As the Bishop's delegate, I present to you this child of fifteen whose entrance you have desired. I trust she may not disappoint your hopes, but I remind you that if it should turn out otherwise, the responsibility will be yours alone."

A chill silence descended on us all. My heart ached for Papa, for I could see that the words of the Canon had struck him to the quick. Yet no one made any reply. After a few more farewells, the door was closed and I was led away. It was time to change my dress of pale blue wool for the black garb of a postulant.

From the beginning, everything about the monastery delighted me. The silence, the poverty, the chanting of the Divine Office, the plain little cell assigned to me, seemed more wonderful than the greatest riches on earth. It was even a cause for joy to be told that I must no longer use the word "my" as I had done in the world. From now on it would be *our* handkerchief, *our* book, *our* cell, since no one in Carmel presumes to claim anything for her exclusive use. Truly I was happy, and not a day passed that I did not rejoice at God's goodness in giving me the vocation to be a Carmelite. I told myself that I was in the monastery forever. Only death could take me away.

Yet I did have troubles. On my entrance I had been assigned some household duties. For a little while each day I worked in the linen room with Mother Mary of the Angels, sub-Prioress and Novice Mistress. I was also given a staircase and a dormitory to sweep. These were only light duties, but being unused to housework I did not always accomplish my tasks properly. One day the Prioress, Mother Mary Gonzaga, discovered a cobweb on the stairway. In the presence of the entire community she gave me a dreadful scolding.

"It's easy to see that our cloisters have been swept by a child of fifteen," she said crossly. "Sister Therese, go and sweep away that cobweb, and learn to be more careful in the future."

I was embarrassed and hurt, too, for never had the Prioress spoken to me sharply. In my visits with her in the parlor, she had always been kind and understanding. From this time on, however, she was continually finding fault. Everything I did was wrong, and presently the Novice Mistress made matters even worse. Almost every afternoon at half-past four she sent me to the garden to do some weeding for exercise. On these little trips I never failed to meet Mother Mary Gonzaga. One day she stopped me, and as usual I could see that she was angry.

"Child, you do absolutely nothing!" she exclaimed. "What kind of a novice are you to have to be sent out every day for a walk?"

I kept silent. A good religious is not expected to make excuses for herself, even when she is in the right. But my heart was heavy many times because of the Prioress' treatment. She no longer seemed to like me. Every time we met I was scolded for being lazy, stupid, slow. Little did I realize that Mother Mary Gonzaga was treating me thus in order to test my vocation, that she really loved me and was doing her best to make me lean upon God instead of upon creatures.

Sometimes Marie and Pauline were irritated with me, too. At recreation time I did not come to sit beside them, but spent this free hour with other nuns instead. I never confided in my big sisters whether I liked being a Carmelite. In spite of their training as religious, they felt that I had changed and no longer loved them as in our days together at home. I was a stranger, not the little girl who had run to them with one childish trouble after another.

I knew what my dear ones were thinking, but did not change my ways. I felt I should not seek for any pleasure, even the most innocent, now that I had come to Carmel to save souls by prayer and sacrifice. That Marie and Pauline sometimes did not understand only made the sacrifice greater and more pleasing to God.

The weeks passed, and I did my best to follow

the Rule. I wanted so much to be a saint! Yet who was there to help and encourage me? Our Lord seemed to have gone very far away. I found it very hard to pray, even at Mass or after Holy Communion. The chaplain and other priests who came to the monastery did not understand what was the matter with me, and when I told one of these, Father Blino, that I wanted to be a saint and to love God as Saint Teresa of Avila had loved Him, he was quite taken back.

"What pride and presumption!" he exclaimed. "Confine yourself to the correction of your faults; see that you offend the good God no more; make some little progress each day, and moderate your rash desires."

I tried to make him understand. "Father, I don't think my desires are rash. Didn't Our Lord say: 'Be ye perfect, as your Heavenly Father is perfect?' "

But Father Blino was not convinced. He repeated his advice, and from then on I was more worried than ever about the state of my soul. Only the chance to speak to another priest, Father Pichon, gave me relief. I had known him before my entrance into Carmel, for he had been confessor to Marie and Pauline, and also the only priest to encourage me to enter the monastery so early. After having heard a general confession of my life, Father Pichon told me to be of good heart for I was in the state of grace. Then he spoke these words:

"In the presence of God, of the Blessed Virgin,

of all the angels and saints, I declare that you have never committed a single mortal sin. Render thanks to the Saviour, Who has given you this grace without any merit on your part."

I was greatly consoled, and promised not to worry any more. There was help from another source, too—that of the reading I was required to do. I already loved one book very much. It was *The Imitation of Christ,* which I knew by heart. But now I began to make a thorough study of the writings of the two great saints of Carmel—Teresa of Avila and John of the Cross. The Bible was given to me also, and I became so attached to the Gospels that when I discovered a volume containing all four, I asked permission to carry it with me always. It was a very tiny book, and so I was able to keep it next to my heart.

Since my entrance, I had worn the black dress and cap of a postulant. As spring gave place to summer, I thrilled at the thought that soon I might exchange this garb for the holy habit of the Carmelite Order. I told myself that generally one remains a postulant for six months. Since I had entered the monastery in April, I would be eligible to become a novice in October — while I was still fifteen. But presently Mother Mary Gonzaga called me aside and said that my Clothing Day would not occur so soon.

"You will have to wait three extra months," she informed me.

There was no explanation for the delay, but

something told me it was not because the Prioress doubted my vocation. No, there was another reason. Perhaps Canon Delatroette did not think I had been tried enough? Perhaps he still believed I had made a mistake in entering a cloistered Order at the age of fifteen?

CHAPTER 9

PRECIOUS CROSSES

FOR some months Papa had not been well. Before my entrance into Carmel, he had suffered a mild attack of paralysis. I had worried about this then, yet still felt I should offer myself to God. Moreover, Celine and Leonie had promised that they would give him good care. There was no real need for me to remain at home.

Through the mercy of God, Papa soon recovered sufficiently to be able to make occasional visits to the monastery. I was always delighted when he came, and so were Marie and Pauline. But one day Papa's visit was made in a more serious mood than usual. He had just returned from a trip to Alencon, our former home.

"My children," he told us, "I received some wonderful graces in the church of Notre Dame. I felt so overwhelmed at God's goodness that I made this prayer: 'My God, it is too much. Yes, I am too happy. It isn't possible to get to Heaven this way. I want to suffer something for You . . .' "

The three of us stared in bewilderment. What did Papa mean? Why was his face now so joyous?

"Children, I offered myself . . . I offered myself as a. . . ."

But the last word would not come, and suddenly we found ourselves supplying it—silently, almost fearfully. In our parish church in Alencon, Papa had offered himself as a victim for sinners!

In the days that followed I pondered upon his revelation very often, and not without sorrow. For years I had prayed for the grace not to give my love to creatures or to try to find happiness in them. Now I glimpsed the truth. God had been pleased with such a prayer, and He had decided to take me at my word. He wanted my whole heart. He wanted to be my only source of happiness, and so He was going to remove the innocent joy of Papa's occasional visits.

Soon this suspicion was confirmed. Papa had another attack of paralysis, from which he recovered only slowly. As I prayed for the grace to accept his illness bravely, to act like a true Carmelite, the Prioress informed me that I would receive the holy habit on January 10, 1889—a week after my sixteenth birthday. And my name in religion, as she had promised me long ago, would be Sister Therese of the Child Jesus.

Once again it was a case of accepting the bitter with the sweet, and I began to prepare for my Clothing Day as fervently as I could. I gave myself and all my actions to Our Lord, sweeping the stairs in His honor, sorting the clothes in the linen room, keeping in good order the little shrine of the Infant Jesus which had been given into my care. In between my work and prayer, however, I thought of a rather unusual favor which I wanted in return.

"Please send some snow on January 10!" I asked Our Lord. "I'm to be dressed as a bride on that day, and I want the whole world to wear white, too!"

It was a childish request, but one on which I had set my heart. After all, I had entered this world when the ground was covered with spotless white, and from childhood snow had charmed me. What if the winter had been a mild one so far? That the possibility of snow was very faint? The Holy Infant would surely give me what I asked, especially since I was going to add His Name to my own on January 10.

"There *will* be snow on my Clothing Day," I told myself. "I just know it!"

The week before my clothing I spent in retreat, praying and thinking about the important step I was to take. Finally came the great day itself. I wore a beautiful dress which Papa had sent, made of white velvet and trimmed with Alencon lace. My hair, hanging in long curls for the last time, was covered with a veil of white tulle and a wreath of lilies. Presently the nuns led me to the cloister door, for according to custom I was to assist at Mass in the public chapel with my family. As I stepped across the threshold, I saw my dear ones waiting for me. Papa was standing just beside the door. His eyes were full of tears as he stretched out his arms and pressed me to his heart.

"Ah, here's my Little Queen!" he murmured. Then as he gave me his hand, we walked together up the center aisle. It was a solemn moment—this last visit to the outside world, this last chance to embrace my beloved father, but again I offered myself to God without reserve. As I assisted at Mass, I told Our Lord I was still His little ball, His toy. He was to do with me as He wished. My one desire was to be united to Him, to be another Christ, a victim for sinners.

When the Holy Sacrifice was over, Papa led me back to the cloister door. Now a lighted candle was in my hand, and I knelt, just as I had done nine months ago, for my father's blessing. A short distance away the Bishop was watching the little scene, and suddenly he intoned the *Te Deum*. This ancient hymn of thanksgiving is truly a glorious one, but it should not have been sung on my Clothing Day. It is reserved only for the day of Religious Profession. But it was too late to do anything about it, and so I re-entered the cloister to the triumphant strains.

IT WAS A SOLEMN MOMENT.

Here the nuns were waiting to lead me to our chapel. As I went down the corridor, I saw the shrine of the Child Jesus, which was my special charge. It was surrounded with lights and flowers, and to my excited eyes the statue of the Holy Infant seemed to smile directly upon me. I smiled in return, then my heart gave a leap of joy. Through the window behind the little shrine I could see snow! Yes—the Child Jesus had heard my prayer, and now the gardens of Carmel were garbed in spotless white in honor of my Clothing Day!

"How wonderful!" I thought. "What human being can make a snowflake fall from Heaven to charm his beloved?"

Presently I was kneeling in the nuns' choir, beside the iron grating which looks out upon the public chapel. The Bishop was already here, waiting to begin the ceremony of reception.

"What do you desire?" he asked.

I knew the answer so well! How many times had I not repeated the wonderful words?

"The Mercy of God, the Poverty of the Order, and the Society of the Sisters," I replied.

Then I was led away from the grating. My white velvet dress was exchanged for the brown woolen habit and cream-colored mantle of the Carmelite Order. My curls were cut, and a white linen veil was placed upon my head. I was a novice at last! God willing, in one more year I would figure in still another ceremony. Before the community assembled in the Chapter Room, I would pronounce the vows of religion. I would make my Religious Profession.

A month after my Clothing Day came the blow I had feared. Papa suffered a third attack of paralysis, and this time there was no recovery. His mind became affected, and presently Celine reported that she and Leonie could no longer look after him. He would have to be placed in an institution.

This was a dreadful cross, one full of suffering and humiliation. Our beloved father was no longer himself! From now on he would have to be cared for by strangers! Quickly I thought of the words Papa had spoken only recently, the words that had told us he had offered himself as a victim for sinners. I thought of something else, too—of that far-off day when I was six years old and had seen the old man walking in our garden with a heavy veil over his head. Had the time finally come for me to understand this strange vision? Yes, I told myself. Papa had joined us in the Carmelite vocation, and therefore we should not grieve over his illness. Rather, we should pray for an increase in faith, so that we might welcome our cross for the great treasure it was.

I tried to express these feelings in a letter to Celine:

> "Far from making any complaint to Our Saviour of the cross He has sent us, I cannot comprehend the infinite love that has urged Him to deal thus with us. Our father must be greatly loved by God, since he has so

much to suffer. What a delight to
share in his humiliation!"

Shortly after my Clothing Day I was given some new duties. No longer was I to work in the linen room with the Novice Mistress. From now on my tasks would lie in the refectory, or dining room. I was to assist Pauline in keeping this room neat and clean, in seeing that places were properly set at mealtime, the glasses filled with water, and bread distributed to each Sister.

Because the will of the Prioress was for each of us the Will of God, I made no comment on this change of tasks. Indeed, some might have thought I had been given a real favor, for now I could spend many hours every day with my "Little Mother". Alas! The new duties brought an unexpected sorrow. Carmelites may speak with one another only twice a day, at recreation, and now it became very difficult for me not to break the Rule. How my heart ached for the chance to talk with Pauline, particularly about Papa! Had she heard any news? Did she think he would be well again some day? Was she still interested in me? Was I doing well as a novice?

But I said nothing. Although the Prioress would readily have granted permission for the two of us to speak, I did not ask for the privilege. Wasn't perpetual sacrifice the mark of life in Carmel? Wasn't it the coin with which sinners could be ransomed? Yes—and I had no desire to let this wonderful coin slip through my fingers.

There was another sacrifice which fell to my lot, one of a totally different nature. It concerned an old nun, Sister Saint Peter, who was badly crippled and needed help to arrive at the refectory. Each evening as we knelt in prayer in the chapel, I would watch for a sign which told me that Sister Saint Peter was ready to be taken to supper. As soon as I saw her shake her hour glass, I would hurry to her side.

I needed a great deal of courage for this task. Sister Saint Peter suffered from rheumatism, which made her cross and irritable, and she was not at all sure that I could lead her safely to the refectory.

"You're too young," she would mumble. "Sixteen years . . . a mere child! You'll walk too fast and I'll fall."

I would smile at the poor old soul and gently help her to her feet. "I'll go very slow," I promised. "Just wait and see, Sister."

Alas! Sister Saint Peter was never satisfied. Either I went too fast and she feared she was going to fall, or I did not go fast enough.

"You're not holding me!" she would exclaim suddenly. "I don't feel your hand! Oh, Sister Therese, I knew you were too young to take care of me properly!"

In such a fashion we made our way to the refectory before the other nuns. But even then my task was not finished. Sister Saint Peter had to be helped into her place in a certain way. Then her sleeves had to be turned back, also in a certain way. All this took much time and patience, but I told myself constantly that Our Lord was living in Sister Saint Peter's soul, despite her whims and uncertain temper. When I was of service to her, I was also of service to Him. Soon it became a real pleasure to stay a while with the poor invalid, to cut her bread for her and search for some other kindness I could render.

So the months passed, and I spent much time pondering over the next great event in my life—the ceremony of Religious Profession. If all went well, it would take place in January, 1890, a year from my Clothing Day. My heart thrilled at the thought and I decided that since I would not be dressed as a bride this time, in lovely white velvet and lace, I would prepare myself another kind of raiment. This would be of the spiritual type, adorned with the jewels and flowers of prayer and sacrifice.

Sacrifice! What greater sacrifice did I have to offer the Heavenly Father than the patient bearing of Papa's illness? But I was constantly in search of others, certainly not as important, but of great value all the same. These were not hard to find, since no anxieties or trials of daily life are too small to be offered to God. For instance, I was often tired and cold. Well, I would offer my discomfort to God the Father, in union with Christ's sufferings and death on Calvary. Then one night I found that someone had taken the little lamp from my cell. For a whole hour I had to sit in the darkness, unable to read as I had planned.

"This is the true meaning of poverty!" I thought. "To be willingly deprived of even the most necessary things for the love of God! Heavenly Father, take this little hardship and turn it into a beautiful jewel for my new dress!"

Some time later there was a chance to make a similar sacrifice. Since my entrance as a postulant, there had been a pretty little jug in my cell which I came to admire very much. One day I saw that it had been taken away and a large jug, much damaged, put in its place. Even as a child I had liked nice things, and I had taken this love for beauty into the cloister. Now, as I looked at the strange and very ugly jug, I knew that here was another chance to show that my thoughts were with God rather than with possessions.

"I won't even look for the pretty jug," I thought. "This old one is better for me."

About this time I experienced an attraction to the Holy Face, for it seemed to me that here was the symbol of every humiliation endured by Our Saviour in the redemption of souls. Most people find it easy to love the little Christ Child, I told myself, but the true Christian never separates Bethlehem from Calvary. Therefore I was delighted when I learned that I might honor the Holy Face in a special way. When the time came for me to make my Profession, I might add a new title to my name in religion and henceforth be known as

Sister Therese of the Child Jesus and of the Holy Face.

Alas! Profession was not to be in January, as I had hoped and prayed, but later in the year—an announcement which filled me with dismay. Since childhood I had felt that I could never belong entirely to God until I had given myself to Him by the vows of poverty, chastity and obedience. Now. . . .

"How long must I wait?" I wondered sadly. "When will my spiritual wedding dress be ready?"

Presently the question was answered. Canon Delatroette had ordered my Profession delayed eight months. He still disapproved of my being in Carmel and would not permit me to make my vows until September 8, 1890. By that time I would be nearing my eighteenth birthday. It was still too early, he thought, and possibly the nuns might yet regret that they had received me into their midst. After all, many girls my age did not know their own minds. They thought themselves suited for this or that life, only to discover later that they had been mistaken.

CHAPTER 10

LIFE IN THE CONVENT

HOW far away the great day seemed now! For eight long and weary months I would have to labor still more on my bridal dress, enriching it as best I could with the beauties of prayer and sacrifice. But I tried to keep the disappointment to myself. After all, the delay must mean that God did not think me worthy of the great privilege of Religious Profession. To comfort myself, I composed a little letter to Our Lord:

> "I no longer ask You to let me make my profession; I shall wait as long as it may please You; but I must not allow my union with You to be delayed by any fault of mine, so will devote all my care to preparing for

> myself a robe enriched with diamonds and every precious stone. When You have found it rich enough, I am sure that nothing will prevent You from taking me as Your spouse."

So the weeks passed, and presently it was September 7, the eve of my Profession. Late that night the community assembled for the chanting of Matins. Afterwards we knelt in silent prayer, waiting for midnight to announce the dawn of the great day. The other nuns were gathered about me, begging God to give me strength and grace for the offering which I was about to make. All was quiet and peaceful in the chapel, when suddenly the beginning of a terrible doubt crept into my mind. Could it be that I was mistaken about my vocation? Perhaps Canon Delatroette had been right, and I did not belong in Carmel. Perhaps I could be of more use to souls by living in the world. Fear swept away my peace, and I could kneel in prayer no longer.

Scarcely knowing what I did, I asked Mother Mary of the Angels, the Novice Mistress, to come out of the chapel with me for a little while. I was so unhappy and frightened that I could not restrain the desire to speak with someone. But when she heard my story, Mother Mary of the Angels just laughed.

"It's the Devil," she assured me kindly. "He doesn't want you to lead a holy life, and so he's trying to tempt you with discouragement. Don't worry, child. This often happens when a novice is about to be professed."

At these words all my anxiety vanished, and the laughter of the Novice Mistress seemed to me the sweetest music in the world. Presently I returned to the chapel, entirely comforted.

The next morning I made my vows, before the community assembled in the Chapter Room. Mother Mary Gonzaga had already told me to ask Our Lord for one special favor on this great day: that of Papa's recovery. I was to make this petition, together with the others I had decided upon, while lying prostrate on the floor.

Now I had already decided not to ask God for this favor. Much as I loved Papa, much as I missed his visits, I did not want him to abandon his own sacrifice as a victim for souls. Apparently it was God's Will that he pass his last years in suffering, and I had learned to rejoice in the fact. Often I told my sisters that Papa's humiliating illness was Our Great Treasure, and we should be duly grateful for it. However, I could not disobey the Prioress, and on the morning of my Profession Day I remembered what she had told me and offered this little prayer:

"My God, grant that Papa may recover if it be truly Your Holy Will."

Then I prayed for Leonie, whose health had been too delicate to endure the hardships of life in a Poor Clare monastery. I asked that she might become a nun in the Visitation Order, and if she did not already have a religious vocation, one might be given to her. I offered many other petitions, too, for I could not bear to forget anyone on this joyous day when I had made a complete offering of myself to God.

"I desire that every sinner on earth may be converted," I told Our Lord, "that Purgatory may no longer hold a single captive. As for myself... may my peace never be disturbed by earthly things. May I be unnoticed and trampled under foot like a little grain of sand. I offer myself to You in order that You may accomplish perfectly Your Holy Will in me, unhindered by any created obstacle."

How happy I was! Throughout the day I wore a crown of roses over my white veil, and when I laid them that night at the feet of the Blessed Virgin I felt that time would never take my joy from me. Now I no longer belonged to myself, only to God. There would be days in the future when sorrow would strike, when life would seem hard and painful, but in the depths of my soul I would be at peace. I had kept nothing back from the Heavenly Father. In return, He would see that I possessed His choicest gifts.

On September 24 I received the black veil—a ceremony which completed my act of Religious Profession. I had hoped that Papa might be well enough to be brought to the monastery on this day, but at the last moment those in charge feared that the excitement would be bad for him. I shed bitter tears of disappointment, even though deep in my heart there was the wonderful peace that comes from knowing one is doing God's Will. When my first grief was past I drew consolation from the fact that now I had a new sacrifice to offer the Heavenly Father, and I rejoiced as I pondered over two sentences which had become very dear to me:

1. *I have come to Carmel to save souls, and more especially to pray for priests.*
2. *I prefer sacrifice to all ecstasies.*

In a letter to Celine, who was feeling lonely and depressed over Papa's continued illness, I tried to be of some comfort:

> "Be consoled! All things pass away, our former life is gone; death will pass, too, and then we shall enjoy life, true life for endless ages, for ever and ever."

After my reception of the black veil, life in the monastery moved along in its usual orderly fashion. I worked and prayed, accepting each hour as a powerful means for saving my soul and the souls of others. Opportunities for sacrifice were never lacking, especially when winter came and the cold seemed to settle in my very bones. Sometimes I could hardly keep my teeth from chattering as we chanted the Divine Office. At night I shivered for hours, so much so that often I could not sleep. Yet God gave me the grace not to complain. He accepted my sufferings, offered in union with those of His Son on Calvary, and applied their merit to souls too lazy or indifferent to pray for themselves.

In the beginning of 1891 I was assigned a new task. No longer would I work with Pauline in the refectory. From now on I was to be assistant sacristan, seeing that the altar linens and the vestments used by the chaplain were kept in good order, the sacred vessels ready for use at the proper time. What joy this new work brought me! I, just eighteen years old, was allowed to touch the chalice in which the Body and Blood of Christ had rested! It seemed too great a privilege, and I often reflected that if I had been born a boy, I should have made every effort to be a priest. What a wonderful vocation, to be able to offer the Holy Sacrifice each day! To absolve poor sinners from their faults, in the Name of Jesus Christ!

Later in the year an influenza epidemic broke out in Lisieux. The dreadful malady struck right and left, finally casting its dark shadow over Carmel. One after another the nuns fell ill, and within a few days three of them were dead—including Mother Mary of the Angels, my former Novice Mistress. I was afflicted, too, but not seriously, and so I was able to give some help as a nurse. These days were filled with death and hardship, but they were made sweet by an unlooked-for privilege. The convent chaplain told me that I might receive Holy Communion each morning during Mass.

To be a daily communicant! I had often prayed for such a grace, but there had never seemed any likelihood of its being granted to me. During the nineteenth century, frequent or daily Communion was not the custom, even in monasteries and convents. Mother Mary Gonzaga had never dreamed of permitting her nuns such a rare privilege, but suddenly, while death and suffering raged about me, the great gift was mine. And without any request on my part.

How happily I approached the Holy Table! What did it matter that often I was tired, that prayer seemed fruitless? I invited all the saints and angels to come and chant their songs of love in my heart. To me it seemed that Our Lord would be pleased with such a joyous welcome. I, too, might share in His joy—no matter how sad and weary I felt.

Even after the epidemic was over, I retained this privilege of receiving Our Lord every day. But finally Mother Mary Gonzaga intervened. It was not proper, she thought, for anyone to be a daily communicant—even a soul vowed to God. As I could not argue with her, I remained away from Holy Communion except on the special feasts when the entire community was allowed to receive Our Lord. Then one day I gave my superior a promise which arose out of the certainty in my own soul.

"You will see, Mother, that I shall make you change your mind about daily Communion after my death."

Mother Mary Gonzaga paid me little heed. To her I was still a child, without experience in either spiritual or worldly matters. Why, my very words revealed it! I was only nineteen, apparently in good health, and I talked of dying! What foolishness! Yet the Prioress did not treat me with all the severity of former years. Sometimes she even seemed to be pleased at my progress as a religious, and presently she assigned me two new duties. I was to do some painting. I was also to try my hand at writing verses. Already Pauline had shown real ability in these accomplishments and possibly I might have a like talent.

I set about these new tasks with great delight. I knew nothing about either one, but God seemed to give me the necessary skill. The holy cards I painted pleased everyone. Pauline was amazed, for she knew I had never had any lessons. Celine was the real artist in our family, having begun a study of art when she was fourteen. She was twenty-three now, and extremely clever with pencil and brush.

As I busied myself with my new tasks, I recalled a little secret I had never told anyone. It concerned the drawing lessons which Celine had been given. I was ten years old when these lessons began, and one day my good father asked me if I would like to learn to draw, too. My eyes had shone at the exciting prospect, and I was just on the point of saying "Yes" when Marie interrupted.

"Therese has no talent for drawing," she said. "Celine is the one who will profit from any lessons."

What a sacrifice to keep silent, not to burst into

eager cries that I might learn drawing, too! Never would I forget the struggle. But grace was provided, and I succeeded so well in hiding my true feelings that no one ever guessed my disappointment. As the months passed, my beloved Celine became really expert with a pencil, while I stood by in silent admiration.

Although I did not have my sister's training, I succeeded in painting a fresco which pleased everyone on the walls of a little oratory. The hymns and verses, dedicated to Our Lord and His Blessed Mother, also gave satisfaction, and frequently I was asked to write a new one for some special feast. There was not much time to devote to writing, and so I tried to arrange my thoughts in rhyme and memorize the result as I swept the floor or worked at other tasks. Then, when I had a few minutes to myself in the evening, I would write down my efforts. The plan worked well, and I was duly grateful.

Mother Mary Gonzaga's term as Prioress came to an end in February, 1893. An election was held to select a new superior and Pauline—Sister Agnes of Jesus—was chosen. At once she appointed Mother Mary Gonzaga as Novice Mistress. To my immense surprise a new duty also came my way. I was to assist Mother Mary Gonzaga in the direction of the novices!

There was considerable amazement in some quarters when my appointment became known. Why, I was only twenty years old! What did I know about the direction of souls? Not so long ago I had been but a novice myself.

Pauline was not disturbed, however. "I have complete confidence in you," she told me. "I know you will not fail."

CHAPTER 11

WRITING DOWN MY CHILDHOOD MEMORIES

SINCE my entrance as a postulant I had been given a variety of tasks. Sweeping, weeding in the garden; working in the linen room, the refectory and the sacristy; painting, writing verses, taking messages from visitors who came to the monastery on business. All these had been little tasks in which I had been able to lean on God in my awkwardness. But to guide souls! How could I, in my great weakness, support others and lead them to Him? I took refuge in prayer. It was as if I threw myself into God's arms like a little child terrified by some fear, who hides his head on his father's shoulder.

"My Saviour," I said, "You see that I cannot feed Your children. If You will to give each what she needs, then fill my hand. Without leaving Your arms, without even turning my head, I shall distribute Your treasures to each soul that comes to me for food. When she finds it according to her taste, she will be indebted to You and not to me. If she finds the nourishment bitter and complains, that will not disturb my peace. I shall try to persuade her that it comes from You, and shall avoid seeking any other for her."

With this prayer on my lips, I entered upon the task assigned to me. Five young girls were in the Novitiate, and it was my duty to see that they understood the meaning of the Carmelite vocation, that they were faithful to the graces given them. From the beginning I impressed upon my charges that they could progress rapidly in the spiritual life if only they would think of themselves as children—*very little children.* They were to put themselves in the arms of the Heavenly Father as I had done. They were not to worry about anything, even as a tiny child is without worries when he feels his father's arms about him. Very soon they would see how such confidence is repaid.

"This is the Little Way to Heaven," I told them. "This is the way that anyone can become a saint."

Although I had made my Profession over two years ago, I remained with the novices and postulants in the Novitiate. Everyone understood that I was only an assistant to Mother Mary Gonzaga, that there was no need to be afraid of me, and so I was treated as a friend and older sister instead of as a superior. From the beginning I found that there was much to do if the five girls under my care were to be properly trained, and so I set about the task of explaining the Little Way as best I could.

This abandonment of oneself as a child into the arms of the Heavenly Father seemed rather strange advice to some of the novices. Surely it was not the way to become a saint. It was too simple, too easy.

"The Little Way is simple, but it is not always easy," I said. "If you follow it, it means giving up your pride. Nothing is harder than that."

There was some disagreement on this point. One novice suggested that the way to become a saint is to say long prayers, to perform difficult sacrifices. To prove her point, she mentioned several holy men and women who had spent their lives in such a manner. Now they were canonized saints.

"That's true," I said. "These good souls went to God by the Great Way. But too many people will never be able to imitate them. For such as these, the Little Way is best."

Presently I was asked how I had chanced upon the Little Way. I smiled at the question, for the answer did not lie in learned books or sermons but in the lessons learned in the days of my babyhood.

"When I was learning to walk, I found it hard to climb the stairs," I said. "I would manage to get up one step; then I would call to my mother. Unless she answered 'Yes, darling,' I would lose

"THE LITTLE WAY IS NOT ALWAYS EASY."

confidence and try no more. But as soon as I heard her voice, I would joyfully scramble up onto the next step. This would be repeated until finally I had climbed all the steps and was in my mother's arms. There were also times when Mama took pity on my poor attempts to reach her arms. Then I did not have to struggle at all. She came down the stairs and carried me with her to the top."

The novices were puzzled. What had such a story to do with the Little Way? Then I told my secret. Climbing stairs is hard for small children, but it is always easy to be *carried* to the top! Then again many rich families have elevators in their homes. Well, I had asked God to give me a very special kind of elevator—His arms!

"Raise your foot in an attempt to mount the stairway of sanctity," I said, "but do not imagine that you will be able to go up even the first step. God only asks for your good intentions. At the top of this stairway, He watches you lovingly. Soon His love will be conquered by your vain efforts, and He will come down Himself to carry you up in His arms."

So we set about the Little Way together, the novices and I, without any trust in our own powers but relying solely on the strength of Our Heavenly Father. We tried to be as much like little children as possible, and, since we were Carmelites, we obeyed our Rule even in trifles. If the bell rang for prayers while we were in the midst of some task, we stopped immediately. If we did not particularly enjoy the company of some Sister, we never showed it. We were even more pleasant to her than to those who attracted us. As a result, we never had to search for means of sacrifice, for they were everywhere about us—ready to be used for the salvation of sinners.

"Since we have placed ourselves in the arms of the Heavenly Father, we must go where He takes us," I said. "Let us always remember this, that we have no will but His. Then nothing can hurt or worry us."

For me, the Little Way was a delight. It meant that I took no credit for any good I was able to accomplish, for any talent I might possess. These were treasures which God had placed in my hand but which were always His. It meant that when I failed in some undertaking, there was no need to be discouraged. Children often fall, but they are too small to hurt themselves seriously. Because I was a child who had given my heart to Him, the Heavenly Father would overlook all my failings.

It was in February, 1893, that I began my work with the novices. A few months later there came the message for which I had prayed long and hard. Leonie announced that she was going to make a second attempt at being a religious. This time she would go to the Visitation nuns in Caen.

How happy I was that one of the most important petitions made on my Profession Day had been granted at last! Of course it was not easy to say good-bye to my beloved sister. Since she was entering a cloistered Order, she would never be able to visit me again. But our hearts were not sad for long, as both of us realized that the present trial would be generously rewarded in Heaven, rewarded far beyond our fondest hopes and dreams.

After Leonie's departure I had the chance to offer still another sacrifice to God. This occurred when Papa was brought to the monastery for a visit with Marie, Pauline and me. We had not seen our good father for several years, since he had been living in an institution, but some time ago he had returned to Lisieux, and now was living with Celine.

How my heart ached as I looked at him! His hair was pure white now, his shoulders bent with age. And he did not seem to recognize his Little Queen! His eyes were glazed, and he could not speak clearly. All he could do was point a trembling hand upwards and mumble two words:

"In Heaven . . . in Heaven. . . ."

I understood, and so did my sisters. Some day Papa would meet us in Paradise. The veil now clouding his mind would be gone forever, and we would be united in unending bliss. Mama would be with us, too, and those four little ones of our family who had died as babies. What happiness for all of us then!

First, however, there must be some suffering. Papa's portion came to an end on July 29, 1894, when he was not quite seventy-one years old. Celine was the only one of us who could attend the funeral, and naturally she was lonely afterwards. Of the five living children of the Martin family, she was the only one remaining in the world.

"Don't worry," I said. "Soon you will come to Carmel, too."

Celine was not sure. She was attracted to the religious life, but did she belong in Carmel? Would she be able to follow such a rigorous Rule? Above all, would the nuns look favorably upon the reception of a fourth member of the same family?

This last objection was not without grounds. Pauline, as Prioress, was willing to accept Celine. Even Mother Mary Gonzaga, the Novice Mistress, made no objections. But there was one particular Sister who was much against her reception. That Celine wished to be a Carmelite was well and good, she said, but let her apply to some other monastery of the Order. Three members of the Martin family were sufficient for the Carmel in Lisieux.

As the weeks passed fresh obstacles arose, and there seemed little likelihood that the Sisters would agree to receive Celine. I was fully resigned to her going to some other Carmel, but something told me that God wished her to be with me. He wished her to learn more about the Little Way than I had been able to relate on her visits in the parlor. Therefore I began to pray with real earnestness for the great favor, and one day after receiving Holy Communion I spoke these words to Our Lord:

> "You know, dear Jesus, how earnestly I have desired that the trials my dear father endured should serve

> as his Purgatory. I long to learn if my wish has been granted, but do not ask that You speak to me. All I want is a sign. You know that one of our community is strongly opposed to Celine's entrance into Carmel. If she withdraws her opposition, I shall look upon it as an answer from You, and in this way shall know if my father went straight to Heaven."

As I left the chapel after my thanksgiving, the first person I met was the Sister in question. There were tears in her eyes, and my heart almost missed a beat as she drew me aside and told me that now she had changed her mind. Henceforth she would do all she could to speed the day of Celine's coming.

I thanked her as well as I could, but all my thoughts were with God. How good He was to His little child! He had let her know that her beloved father went straight to Heaven. Then He had granted her second request and removed the chief obstacle to Celine's entrance.

Presently I wrote to my sister:

> "This is perhaps the last time, my dear little sister, that my pen must serve me for a talk with you; the good God has granted my wish.... Our dear father is making us feel his presence in a way that is profoundly touching. After five long years of deathlike separation, what joy to find him as of old, and even more fatherly. Oh, how well will he repay you for

> all your care of him! You have been his angel; he will now be yours. See, he has not yet been a month in Heaven, and already by his powerful intercession all your projects succeed. It is now easy for him to arrange what concerns us, and therefore has he had less trouble for Celine than he had for his poor Little Queen."

A few weeks later, on September 14, 1894, Celine came to join us in Carmel. I embraced her eagerly, a privilege which had been denied me for over five years. Then I remembered that it was hardly fitting to show too much interest in one of my own relatives. Now that four of us were living under the same roof, there was the possibility of leading too much of a family life. Therefore I was about to withdraw when Pauline, using her authority as Prioress, set aside my intended sacrifice.

"Take Celine to her cell," she told me. "From now on she will be one of your charges."

From the beginning my beloved sister did well as a postulant and understood, perhaps better than the others in the Novitiate, the remarkable value of the Little Way. She followed my advice and gave herself into the arms of the Heavenly Father with complete trust. How my heart rejoiced at this, for now I knew that Celine's happiness was assured. What if sorrows did come, and trials? She would still experience the wonderful peace which comes to those who have abandoned themselves to God as little children.

One evening at recreation, during the Christmas season of this same year, I had the happy opportunity of spending a little while with Marie and Pauline. Such occasions were few and far between, for in a convent one should not have special friends or companions. I had always tried to be faithful to this rule, and therefore the few times when I spoke privately with my sisters were cause for real joy. In fact, my heart overflowed with such happiness on this particular occasion that it seemed very natural to recall other times when we had been together with our loved ones. For instance, did Pauline remember how I had chosen her to be my "Little Mother" after Mama's death? Did Marie remember how she had asked the Blessed Virgin to cure me of my illness?

As she listened to my eager descriptions of our life together, first in Alencon, then in Lisieux, a host of happy memories flooded Marie's soul. Later she took Pauline aside and asked a most unusual favor.

"Mother Prioress, why don't you tell Sister Therese to write down these childhood memories? I think her words would be very helpful to others."

Pauline was amazed at this request from Sister Mary of the Sacred Heart. Wasn't Sister Therese already surrounded with a multitude of duties? And what possible value could her childhood memories have for others?

"They would show what wonderful parents we had," protested Marie, "how we learned everything good from them. Oh, Mother Prioress, I'm very sure such a story would be worthwhile!"

Pauline hesitated, but when a few days had passed she summoned me to her cell and announced that I was to write the story of my life. It was to be finished in one year's time—on January 21, 1896, the feast of Saint Agnes.

"That will be my feast day," said Pauline kindly. "You may bring your little book to me then as a gift."

I was amazed at such an assignment, yet since it was given to me by the Prioress it was clearly given to me by God, too. A few days later I knelt before the statue of Our Lady which once had smiled on me and asked the Queen of Heaven to bless my new work. I begged her to guide my hand so that I should not pen a single line that would not be pleasing to her. Then I opened the New Testament.

"What shall I call my story?" I wondered. "What would be a good title?"

Suddenly my eyes fell upon this sentence from the Gospel of Saint Mark: *"Jesus, going up a mountain, called to Him men of His own choosing."*

I was delighted at the wonderful simplicity of these words. How exactly they applied to my own life! From the heights of Heaven, God had chosen me for His own. More than that. Knowing my weakness, *He had come down to get me!*

As I reflected upon the wonder of it all, my thoughts turned to the evening when I had told Papa of my vocation to Carmel. He had been so kind, so understanding. He had picked a little white lily and explained that its purity was like that of my soul. If I wished to give myself to God, small and unstained, nothing could please him more. I still had the little white lily, a precious souvenir of that wonderful night.

Suddenly all doubts as to the title of my new work vanished. Pauline had told me to describe my childhood. Well, I would do just that. So without hesitation I began to write these words: *The Story of the Springtime of a Little White Flower.*

CHAPTER 12

MY LITTLE WAY

I was twenty-two years old when I set about writing my childhood memories for Pauline. No special time had been granted me for this task, but I managed to find a couple of hours each day. Two notebooks, such as children use in school, were given to me for my work, and by summertime I had written several thousand words.

How my heart overflowed as I related the story of my life! More than ever I realized God's goodness in providing me with two saints for parents, a comfortable home, love and affection from relatives and friends. Millions of little ones were deprived of such blessings, yet from the beginning they had been mine. More than that. Papa and Mama had always appreciated the value of a religious vocation. They had asked for this great grace for each of their children, and the fact that five of us were now in the convent, saving our own souls and the souls of others, was a further proof of God's goodness.

"Heavenly Father, You have been so generous!" I would exclaim, over and over again. "Now I want to give You something in return."

But what could I give, I asked myself, I who was so little and weak? For some time I prayed and reflected, and then the inspiration came. Already I was following the Little Way of childlike trust and surrender to God's Will. Now I would offer myself to the Heavenly Father in a new fashion. I would make myself a victim of His love.

It was one day during Mass when I made this Act of Love for the first time. Later I sought out Pauline and asked her approval of what I had done. She did not seem to attach much importance to the matter, and readily gave her permission for me to repeat my offering. Then I put the Act of Love in writing and submitted it to a priest who was preaching our retreat. He also approved, and so I made the Act once more—solemnly, this time—on the Feast of the Most Holy Trinity, June 9, 1895. Then I placed the paper on which the precious words were written in the little book of Gospels, next to my heart.

My Act of Love was rather long, but it was based on a simple fact. People are afraid of God, I told myself. They look on Him as a distant Being Who permits suffering and sorrow, Who punishes even the smallest sin. Because of this, death is something to be dreaded and Heaven almost impossible of attainment. But gradually I had been given the grace to realize that God is as much a Being of love and mercy as He is of justice. He has an infinite love for mankind, and most of the time this love finds no appreciation. People are too busy loving creatures and possessions to think of the immense love God has for them.

The desire to atone for these souls who refuse to accept God's love, who cruelly neglect Him year after year, led me to offer myself as a victim of this same love. I asked God to shower me with *all* His love, even to the point where I could not bear such tenderness. I would die then, of course, as much a martyr as though I had given my life in defense of the Faith.

As a result of this offering, wonderful graces were soon flooding my soul. One day, while I was making the Stations of the Cross, I experienced the penetration of a heavenly flame that seemed to pierce my very being. What pain! What sweetness! Truly the Hand of God was upon me, and I thought I was dying. But in an instant the invisible fire was gone and I was left to ponder upon its meaning. Was this a sign that God planned to take me to Heaven soon? Surely it was, for I had always believed my earthly life would be a short one. The little white flower would flourish in its springtime only.

"What does it matter if my life is long or short?" I thought. "I fear only one thing: it is to keep my own will. Dear God, take that! I choose everything that You have decided for me!"

This year of 1895 was an important one. Not only did it witness the beginning of the little book for Pauline and the Act of Love. It also brought the entrance into Carmel, on August 15, of my beloved cousin, Marie Guerin. Years ago we had been students at the Benedictine convent. We had also shared happy days at the seashore. Then there were other childhood memories, particularly those of playing as hermits at *The Elms*. (Also in the streets of Lisieux on one memorable occasion!) Now my prayers were answered at last. God had granted Marie the grace to work for Him as a Carmelite—as Sister Mary of the Eucharist. He willed that she should be with me in the Novitiate where I might explain the beauty of the Little Way.

Two months later a most astonishing thing happened. I was helping in the laundry when Pauline sent word for me to come to her. She had just received a letter from a young seminarian, a member of the Society of the White Fathers. He expected to be ordained in a few years, then leave for Africa as a missionary. But although he was happy to work for God, he dreaded being separated from his family. He wished to be a saint, yet he was fearful of the sacrifices that might be in store for him. Sometimes he even wondered if he should continue his studies for the priesthood.

"You may write to this young man and encourage him," Pauline told me. "It will do him good to have a little sister in Carmel who prays and suffers for his intentions."

I was delighted with the assignment, for everything pertaining to the priesthood was close to my heart. After all, had I not come to Carmel to ask God to bless the world with many good and holy priests? As for the Foreign Missions, would I not willingly give my life, endure any suffering, in order that some poor pagan might embrace the True Faith?

"This seminarian needs to learn about the Little Way," I thought. "He is full of doubts and worries now because he is relying on his own strength. I will tell him to forget all these. When he has put himself as a little child in the arms of the Heavenly Father, things will be so different!"

My new brother seemed to appreciate my letters and to profit from them, too. In a little while I decided to ask him a favor. Each day he was to address the following petition to Heaven:

> *"Merciful Father, in the Name of Your sweet Jesus, of the Holy Virgin and all the saints, I ask You to inflame my sister with Your spirit of Love, and to give her the grace to make You greatly loved."*

The young seminarian agreed to say this prayer daily for the rest of his life. He would never forget it, he told me, or the Little Way to Heaven which

I had taught him. I made the same request of a second brother who was given to me some months later. He was already a priest, and one day he came to the monastery and offered the Holy Sacrifice. I had the opportunity to speak with him twice on this day, and I gave him my promise that I would offer my prayers and sufferings for the success of his missionary work in China. In return he was to ask God to allow me to bring many souls to Him, even after my death.

How grateful I was for this chance to play some little part in the work of Christ's apostles! Because I was a girl, I could never be a priest. Because I was a cloistered nun, I could never teach the truths of our Holy Faith in pagan lands. Yet I could still have some share in both missions. Through hidden prayer and sacrifice I could merit for both my brothers the strength to carry on their difficult labors. United with Christ, a trusting child in the arms of my Heavenly Father, I could be the channel through which this grace would flow.

I continued to work on my little story for Pauline, and on January 20, 1896, the eve of Saint Agnes, it was completed. That night as I went to chapel for prayer, I paused a moment beside my beloved sister and gave her the manuscript. She acknowledged the gift with a nod but did not speak. Then I retired, trusting that *The Story of the Springtime of a Little White Flower* would prove satisfactory. I felt that it was no literary masterpiece. It was only eight chapters in length and written on very poor paper. I had not bothered to correct it or to make any changes, and nowhere had I made an effort to be amusing or clever. However, Pauline might find pleasure in reading about the wonderful favors God had granted me during my short life.

Time passed, and my sister made no comment on the story of my childhood memories. The truth was that she had not found time to read it. Her term as Prioress expired in February, 1896, and she was anxious to set everything in order for her successor. This successor turned out to be Mother Mary Gonzaga, who had been Prioress at the time of my entrance. There was every chance that now I would be given new duties, but as it turned out I was told to continue working with the novices. I might also help the Sister who had charge of the sacristy, as I had done in the past.

The spiritual guidance of the novices was a work dear to my heart. I saw in these young souls the future welfare of our monastery—indeed, the future welfare of countless men and women we should never know. I did my best to teach my little sisters one important fact: namely, that each and every soul born into the world is called to be a saint—not by halves, not with indifference, but totally, and with joy. For some the process is long and difficult, chiefly because such persons rely on their own powers and do not think of abandoning themselves to the Heavenly Father with confidence and trust. Others achieve sanctity more quickly because they have learned to be humble.

"When I think of all I still have to acquire!" cried a novice one day, a bit depressed over her struggles to become virtuous.

"You mean all that you have to lose," I said. "You are trying to climb a mountain, whereas God wishes you to *descend.*"

Yes, *descend* was one of my favorite words. So were *little* and *humble* and *child.* Over and over again I described the beauty of simplicity in one's spiritual life. It is such a sure way to God! It leads straight to His Heart, I explained, without any twistings or turnings. Only when we cease to be simple and childlike do things become hard for us.

Since I was not their real superior, the novices were not backward in criticizing some of my statements. One or two did not take kindly to being as little children, for by now they had found that this practice requires constant effort. It is no lazy man's way to Heaven, since it means accepting suffering and humiliation without complaint. These, as well as joy and earthly fortune, are gifts from the Heavenly Father for the good of one's soul and the souls of others.

"I just don't like to suffer and to be humiliated," complained one. "I'm very sure the cross will never attract *me.* Sister Therese, how can I be a saint with such feelings?"

I did my best to explain that *feelings* do not matter, that this novice could make a very wonderful prayer out of her dislike for suffering and humiliation. She could present it to the Heavenly

Father as a token of her weakness. In such a way would she be true to her role of a little child.

"If you feel regret that all the flowers of your desires and of your good intentions fall to the ground without producing any fruit, offer to God this sacrifice of never being able to gather the fruit of your efforts. In an instant, at the hour of your death, He will cause the very best fruit to ripen on the tree of your souls."

The novice was somewhat consoled, but I knew what she was thinking. Sister Therese of the Child Jesus and of the Holy Face offered such strange advice! Never had her Little Way been praised or even mentioned by the priests who gave our retreats, and yet she did not seem concerned. Instead, she acted as though things would be quite different some day. Then the whole world would accept her words, and practice what she taught.

CHAPTER 13

A WONDERFUL DREAM AND A TERRIBLE TEMPTATION

PRESENTLY it was the Lenten season of 1896. As is the custom in Carmel, many additional prayers and sacrifices were offered to the Heavenly Father at this time. Often I was quite tired after a long day, but sufficient strength was still present so that I did not ask to be excused from any duties. Indeed, most of the time I enjoyed a sense of perfect health, and on the night of Holy Thursday, April 3, when several of the other nuns received permission to watch until dawn at the Repository, it was a bit of a disappointment to learn that I had been overlooked. Apparently Mother Mary Gonzaga did not think I would be strong enough for the customary exercises of Good Friday if I spent the whole night in prayer.

Long ago I had learned the merit of obedience, and so about midnight I left the chapel without reluctance and went to my cell. I lighted the lamp and spent a few minutes preparing for bed. Then I put out the flame and lay down. But no sooner had I done so than I experienced the strangest feeling. A hot stream had risen to my lips, and I felt as though I was dying!

"What is it?" I thought. "What's wrong?"

It would have been perfectly proper to light the lamp again and find out, but I decided against it. After all, it was Lent—a period when every Christian is meant to do extra penance for his sins.

"Here is a chance to mortify my curiosity," I told myself. "I shall wait until morning to see what's happened."

Without thinking more about this unexpected sacrifice, I settled myself on the bed and very soon was sound asleep. However, when the rising bell awakened me at five o'clock, my first thought was one of pleased expectation. I remembered that I had something to discover. Quickly I looked for my handkerchief, then smiled at what I saw. Yes—my suspicions of the night before had been right. The white handkerchief was stained with blood!

"*Tuberculosis!*" I thought. "*I have it!*"

Far from feeling sad or frightened, I recognized my condition with real joy. Tuberculosis is a very serious disease of the lungs. Many times people recover from it, but I felt sure that I would not. In a few months, in a year or two at the most, the little white flower would be gathered to its Creator. On this Good Friday, the anniversary of Christ's own death, she had heard the first call to the heavenly harvest.

Later in the day I sought out Mother Mary Gonzaga and told her what had happened. She looked me up and down, then asked how I felt.

"I feel perfectly fine, Mother. Not a bit sick."

After some thought, Mother Mary Gonzaga then gave me permission to finish Lent as I had begun. I might fast on bread and water throughout Good Friday. I might go to the chapel with the others. And if I felt strong enough to do some work....

"I feel strong enough for anything!" I cried joyfully.

The Prioress agreed that I looked unusually well. There was a really good color in my cheeks.

"I guess it will be all right for you to wash the windows," she said. "We want to have things clean for Easter."

I followed the Good Friday observances with great zest, but after a few hours real fatigue came upon me. One of the novices uttered a cry of alarm when she found me washing windows and all but fainting at the task.

"Why, Sister Therese, you're as pale as death! You must be ill!"

I shook my head. "I'm all right," I said, trying to give her a reassuring smile. "Sister, you mustn't imagine things."

THE PRIORESS THOUGHT I LOOKED UNUSUALLY WELL.

The novice was not convinced and begged me to allow her to inform the Novice Mistress as to my condition. Surely I ought to be in bed instead of washing windows! And surely I should have a nourishing meal. . . .

"Please don't bother the Novice Mistress," I said. "Or anyone else. I may look a little tired, but I'm quite all right."

Seeing that I would not give her the desired permission, the novice withdrew. I could tell she was worried, and immediately I decided that I must not alarm anyone else. If Marie, Pauline or Celine suspected that I was ill, they would be very disturbed. In one sense the joyful feast of Easter would be spoiled for them.

For some weeks I succeeded in keeping the symptoms of my illness from my sisters, but then I fell prey to a bad cough. It was impossible to control this, and soon Mother Mary Gonzaga was really worried. She sent for Doctor de Cornière, who usually attended us in case of illness, and also for Doctor La Néele, who some years ago had married my cousin, Jane Guerin. Both physicians agreed that I must stop work at once and go to bed. I must eat plenty of good food and take the medicines they ordered. Since I was only twenty-three, there was every chance that I could overcome my illness.

Although this report meant that my going to Heaven might be delayed, I rejoiced for one reason. Mother Mary Gonzaga had promised that if I recovered, she would send me on a wonderful mission. I was to go to the Carmel in Hanoi, in French Indo-China, where the nuns were in need of helpers. Of course it would mean saying good-bye to my three beloved sisters, to my cousin Marie, but what joy would be mixed with the sacrifice! For years God had flooded my soul with graces of all kinds. In the world I had been surrounded with love and affection, with earthly comforts. In Carmel even greater happiness had come my way. But now I was to go to a foreign land where no one knew or loved me. I was to be an exile, with untold opportunities to suffer for others.

"Dear Lord, if it is Your Will that I know this new kind of sacrifice," I prayed, "how happily shall I receive it!"

It was some time later, on the night of May 10, that I had a surprising dream. I thought that I was walking along the corridor with the Prioress. Suddenly I perceived three strange nuns ahead of me, dressed in the Carmelite habit. Their veils were lowered, and immediately I experienced a great desire to know who they were.

"I think these Sisters come from Heaven," I told myself. "Oh, if I could see the face of just one of them!"

As though I had spoken aloud, the tallest of the three nuns began to come toward me. I fell on my knees, then gasped with astonishment as she raised her veil and looked at me tenderly. It was none other than Mother Anne of Jesus, a companion of

Saint Teresa of Avila and the first to bring the Carmelite Reform to France!

How it was that I recognized the saintly religious I could not tell. I had never had any special devotion to her, although I had read about her holy life and knew that she had died in 1621. But there was no doubt in my mind as to her identity. Her face was beautiful with a beauty not of this earth. As I knelt before her, she dropped her veil about me and caressed me with great affection. Feeling myself so loved, I found courage to speak:

"Oh, Mother! Is God going to leave me long on this earth or is He coming for me soon?"

Mother Anne smiled. "Yes, soon . . . soon . . . I promise you . . . "

"Does He require nothing more of me than my poor little acts and desires? Is He satisfied with me?"

Suddenly the face of the saintly nun shone with even greater tenderness. "God asks nothing more of you," she said. "He is pleased . . . very pleased . . ."

As she spoke, she took my head between her hands and kissed me so lovingly that no words can convey the sweetness of her embrace. My heart was full of joy and I thought of my sisters. Surely Mother Anne would be pleased to make them happy, too. Perhaps she would grant some favor . . . some grace . . . But as I was trying to decide what I should ask, the dream vanished and I awoke to find myself staring at the bare walls of my little cell.

For weeks afterwards the memory of this dream brought me joy. It confirmed the belief I had always had, that I should die while still young. What if the doctors insisted that I was going to get well, that the warm spring days were causing a remarkable improvement in my health? Deep in my heart was the certainty that God thought me nearly ready for the wonderful reward He had prepared for me in Heaven.

At first no one shared this opinion. I was allowed to get out of bed and try my hand at a few light tasks, such as mending, writing verses and painting holy cards. Later on, however, my sisters began to suspect the truth, and one September day Marie asked me a favor.

"You wrote your childhood memories for Pauline," she told me. "Now will you please write something for me? You see, I don't have your desires for suffering and humiliation. I cannot bring myself to pray for them. And when I hear you speak of wanting to be a martyr . . . to suffer all manner of deaths for Christ . . . oh, little sister, *please* help me!"

When Mother Mary Gonzaga had given the necessary permission, I set about the task of consoling my beloved godmother.

"My desire for martyrdom counts for nothing," I wrote. "That is not the reason why God takes pleasure in my little soul. What pleases Him is the fact that I love my littleness and my poverty, and that I have a blind trust in His Mercy."

I reminded Marie, as I had so often reminded the novices, that pious feelings are of little importance. God has no need of pious feelings, or even of pious works. His one desire is that we trust Him as a little child trusts his father, and that we love Him with all our hearts. Then I wrote a sentence which described the state of my own soul since the previous Easter:

"My consolation is to feel that I have none on earth."

Hardly anyone would have understood what I meant by this. They saw me smiling, apparently happy in spite of my illness. They heard me speak of trust and confidence, of surrender to God's Will, of the reward awaiting those who do that Will. They did not dream that recently I had been sent a terrible trial. Yes—it was now very difficult for me to believe my own words. I was almost overwhelmed by doubts as to the existence of God, of Heaven, of anything save a dark nothingness beyond the grave. Sometimes it seemed that I could even hear the Devil laughing at my poor efforts to be a saint.

"Continue as you are doing," he would say. "Rejoice in death, which will not give you the joy for which you hope but the night of nothingness!"

How terrible was this temptation against faith! Sometimes I reflected how millions of people have given in to it—laughing at the idea of there being a God, a Heaven, a life beyond the grave. I shuddered at the thought, and then with all my strength offered this little prayer:

> "Lord, Your child asks pardon for her unbelieving brethren. For love of You will she sit at that table of bitterness where poor sinners take their food; she has no wish to rise from it until You give the sign. But may she not say in her own name and in the name of her guilty brethren: 'Oh, God, be merciful to us sinners! Send us away justified. . . .' "

Although I had not the consolations of faith, I forced myself to perform works in accordance with faith. In the first year of my illness, I made more Acts of Faith than in my whole previous life. I continued to write about the beauties of Heaven and the eternal possession of God, but now I was writing only of that which I willed to believe. The night of the spirit had become not a curtain but a wall between Heaven and me.

This temptation against faith was confided to the Prioress and the convent chaplain, but to no one else. Indeed, the other nuns would have been very much startled if they had known that Sister Therese of the Child Jesus was afflicted in such a manner. Why, this little nun was always counseling others to look upon God as a Father of love and mercy. She was smiling and gay, despite her recent illness. Not a day passed that she did not have some word of encouragement for others. Truly, she acted like a little child. What was more natural than that she should be preserved from every hardship?

I rejoiced that the community was unaware of the real state of my soul, for sufferings borne in secret are of extreme value in helping others. Besides, had I not often prayed to be a martyr? Even at the age of fourteen, when Celine and I had kissed the holy ground of Rome, I had asked for this grace. On my Profession Day I had repeated the request.

"Grant me martyrdom of heart or body!" I had prayed. "Ah, rather, give me both!"

However, the thought sometimes occurred that I was being selfish in wishing to die young. Who was I, who told others to abandon themselves into the arms of the Heavenly Father, to choose what was or was not best?

"Maybe God wishes to cure me and let me go to Hanoi after all," I told myself. "Maybe He wishes me to ask for this grace."

In November of 1896 I began a novena to one of my special friends, Blessed Theophane Venard. This holy priest had died a martyr's death in China in 1861, and I was very much attracted to him after reading the story of his life. He had been such a simple and trusting soul, so cheerful and fond of his family. He had never heard of my Little Way, and yet he had followed it. Humbly I asked the favor that I might go to the Orient, too—if this was God's Will. But the novena was scarcely finished when I fell ill again. A new weakness settled in my bones, and it was only with the greatest difficulty that I could drag myself about. God had blessed my desire for suffering, however, and so He arranged that the Prioress should consider me to be in much better health than I actually was. I was allowed to work as usual, in the laundry and elsewhere, and since my cell was somewhat apart from the others, no one was disturbed by my coughing at night.

How tired I was when the hours of prayer and work were finished at last! It took me a long, long time to climb the stairs to my cell, and even longer to get ready for bed. When I did lie down, I was often unable to sleep. It was so cold and damp in the little cell! And because I wished to suffer all I could for souls, I would not ask for more blankets. Many times I felt that it was only God's power which kept me from dying of the cold. Ever since I had come to Carmel, this had been one of my greatest sufferings.

It was some weeks later, shortly after my twenty-fourth birthday, when Mother Mary Gonzaga suddenly realized the seriousness of my condition. At once she summoned the doctors, but this time they shook their heads when asked for an opinion.

"There is little we can do for Sister Therese," they said gravely. "She has only a few months to live."

CHAPTER 14

MYSTERIOUS PROMISES

WHEN my three sisters and my cousin heard the report, their hearts were heavy. Why had I kept my illness a secret? Why had I not confided in them? Quickly I explained that I had not wished to cause them any anxiety, but these words did not satisfy my dear ones.

"You must go to the Infirmary at once," declared Marie. "You need all the care and comfort we can give you."

My dear godmother meant well, but I was happy when the Prioress told me that I might remain in my cell. This little room, cold and damp as it was, had been home to me ever since I entered the monastery. Here I had learned to pray and suffer as a Carmelite, and here I hoped to give up my soul to God. Besides, spring was at hand, the spring of 1897, and the cold days were almost over.

The doctors had ordered treatments to relieve my coughing spells, and I did my best to submit with good grace. But the treatments were so painful! And the medicines prescribed, so unpleasant!

"It's a waste of time and money," I told myself. "I know I am going to die soon."

To die! This would mean the end of all suffering, I reflected, and the beginning of the only life that counts. When I was dead, my body would be carried to the nuns' chapel and placed before the large iron grating which looks out upon the public church. A wreath of roses would be on my head, and the people of Lisieux would come to stare through the iron bars at Sister Therese of the Child Jesus and of the Holy Face. The Prioress would send a circular letter to all the Carmels in France, giving a brief description of my life and death. After a day or so, my body would be taken away from the monastery and buried in the town cemetery. Of course my relatives and sisters in religion would remember me in prayer, but after a few months there would be few to think upon the little white flower.

"Only You will not forget me, Lord," I said. "You never forget anybody!"

One day as I was resting after a very painful treatment, I heard a kitchen Sister speaking in the corridor outside my cell. There was real concern in her voice.

"Sister Therese is going to die soon," she said, "and I've been asking myself what Mother Prioress can possibly say about her in the circular letter. I think she will be very embarrassed."

"Why?" asked another voice.

"Well, this little Sister is very amiable, but surely she has done nothing much since coming here."

I smiled at the truth in these words. The kitchen Sister was so right! Never had I done anything of myself, in the world or as a nun. Always my lot had been to remain in the arms of the Heavenly Father, small and weak, relying upon His love to help me become a saint.

Since my entrance into Carmel, I had never sought consolation and companionship from Marie and Pauline, nor of Celine and Marie Guerin when they joined us. But now that I knew my days were numbered, I made no effort to deny myself this very natural joy. Every day my beloved ones came for a visit, and presently Pauline astonished me by presenting herself with pencil and paper. It seemed that she wished to record a few of my sayings which she thought would be helpful to the Sisters.

At first I was disturbed at this. Who was I to give advice to others? Yet since Pauline had her heart set on it, I finally agreed. A few weeks later she informed me that if I felt strong enough, it might be well to add some extra chapters to my book, *The Story of the Springtime of a Little White Flower.*

"Mother Prioress has given permission for this work," she told me. "My dear, I do hope you can do it."

By now it was the month of June, and sunshine flooded every corner of the monastery. I felt a little better, and I promised to do my best.

"But what shall I write about?" I asked. "Surely I have told everything about my childhood."

"Write about the novices, or about charity," suggested Pauline.

Charity! This was a theme which had always been very dear to me. Years ago I had memorized that wonderful letter written by Saint Paul to his friends in Corinth, and now the words returned in all their original strength:

> "If I speak with the tongues of men, and of angels, and have not charity, I am become as sounding brass or a tinkling cymbal. And if I should have prophecy and should know all the mysteries, and all knowledge, and if I should have all faith, so that I could remove mountains, and have not charity, I am nothing. And if I should distribute all my goods to feed the poor, and if I should deliver my body to be burned, and have not charity, it profiteth me nothing. Charity is patient, is kind; charity envieth not, dealeth not perversely; is not puffed up; is not ambitious, seeketh not her own, is not provoked to anger, thinketh no evil; rejoiceth not

> in iniquity, but rejoiceth with the truth; beareth all things, hopeth all things, endureth all things. Charity never falleth away . . ."

"I will do my best to write on charity," I thought. "Dear Lord, please help me!"

In the days that followed, I wrote about fifty pages on that greatest of all virtues. I tried to describe my own poor efforts to acquire this beautiful jewel. Frequently, however, I had to interrupt my writing to smile. My methods of practicing charity were so unusual! For instance, whenever I found it difficult to be kind to some Sister, to refrain from showing impatience because her ways irritated me, *I would run away from her as quickly as I could!* Then there was the case of a companion who annoyed me by rattling her beads when we were at meditation. The sound was so irritating that many times I felt like turning around and giving her a sharp look. But for the sake of charity I adopted another method. Instead of trying to escape the unwelcome noise, I would set myself to listen to it as though it were the sweetest music. As a result, my meditation became not a period of peace and quiet but time spent in offering "music" to Our Lord.

Another opportunity to practice charity was sometimes provided in the laundry. One day as I was scrubbing clothes, I was startled by a splash of dirty water across my face. I looked quickly at the Sister who was scrubbing vigorously at my side.

My first impulse was to pause and deliberately wipe away the water from my face. This would show her what I thought of her carelessness. But my irritation did not last. Instead of having my little revenge, I set myself to welcome each splash of soapy water as though it were a treasure. Soon the unpleasantness crept away, and my heart was full of the peace that always springs from genuine kindness.

The first chapters of *The Story of the Springtime of a Little White Flower* had been dedicated to Pauline, Sister Agnes of Jesus. Later, Marie had asked for further explanations of the Little Way, and so I had written a chapter for her, Sister Mary of the Sacred Heart. Now I decided to dedicate the new chapters on charity to our Prioress, Mother Mary Gonzaga. Despite her severe treatment of me when I first came to the monastery, I had always loved her deeply. One day I found myself writing these lines:

> "When I was a postulant there were times when I was so violently tempted to seek my own satisfaction, some crumbs of pleasure, by having a word with you, that I was obliged to hurry past your cell and cling to the banisters to keep myself from turning back. Many were the permissions I wanted to ask, and pretexts for yielding to my natural affection sug-suggested themselves by the hundreds . . ."

No, life in Carmel had not been easy for a fifteen-year-old girl—especially one with a sensitive heart and a real capacity for love. How well I recalled those days when I would cling to the banisters to keep myself from running to the Prioress for advice and consolation! And how hard it had been not to talk at will with Marie and Pauline! At the time I had told myself that they were my sisters and that I was entitled to some special place in their affections. It was my *right*, and I was doing something really noble in not attempting to enjoy it. How pleased God must be with me!

Alas! Such feelings were mine because I was making the mistake that most people make. I thought I had rights to this or that privilege, when actually I had no rights at all. I had forgotten, perhaps for just a little while, that I was only a poor creature who owed her very existence to God's love.

"I hope I'm wiser now," I thought to myself. And then I reflected upon a favorite theme: people cannot be free or happy until they have renounced all claims to freedom and happiness. Only when they have seen themselves as little children, depending on God's mercy for the very air they breathe, can they find peace.

As the month of June came to an end, I found myself growing very weak. No longer had I the strength to dip my pen into the ink, and so I used a pencil for my writing. But finally even this effort proved too much. I could work no more on the story of my life. By July it was even too difficult for me to walk to my invalid chair under the chestnut trees in the garden.

"Now it *is* time for you to go to the Infirmary," said Pauline.

I was silent. What good was rest to me now, or other bodily comforts? On July 8, as I said good-bye to my poor little cell, my heart filled with a sudden emotion.

"When I am in Heaven, you must bear in mind that a great part of my happiness was won in this little cell," I told Pauline. "I have suffered greatly here. I would have liked to die here."

Very slowly Pauline led me to the Infirmary, for by now the least effort caused me great pain. When we arrived, I saw that the statue of the Blessed Virgin which had smiled upon me over fourteen years ago had been placed beside the bed. I paused to look at it lovingly.

"What do you see?" asked Marie, her voice vibrant with hope.

"I see the statue, and never has it appeared so beautiful. But before, as you well know, it was not the statue."

My dear godmother sighed. She had been praying so earnestly that I would see the Blessed Virgin again, that she would smile and cure me!

A week later Pauline produced her pencil and paper and sat down beside my bed. She believed that I was now uttering statements which were in some measure directly inspired by the Holy Ghost and which ought therefore to be exactly recorded. Certainly there was something very unusual about my words. For instance, although I knew I was going to die I still insisted that my work on earth was far from being completed. Rather, it was close at hand.

"I feel that my mission is soon to begin," I said, "my mission to make the good God loved as I love Him, to give to souls my Little Way. If the good God grants my desires, my Heaven will be spent upon earth until the end of the world. *Yes, I will spend my Heaven in doing good upon earth....* I shall not be able to rest until the end of the world. But when the Angel shall have said, 'Time is no more,' then I shall rest. I can then enjoy repose, for the number of the elect will be complete and all will have entered into eternal bliss."

"By what way do you wish to lead souls?"

"By the way of spiritual childhood, the way of confidence and self-surrender. I wish to show them the Little Way that has so perfectly succeeded with me...."

Dear Pauline! How carefully she wrote down my words, feeling that some day they would be useful to others! When she had left my side, she would read them over and over again, to make sure that nothing had been omitted. Marie and Celine were also interested in the strange remarks I made, and faithfully reported them. For instance, not so long ago Marie had told me that she felt there would be great sorrow in the Sisters' hearts when I left them for Heaven.

"Oh, no!" I had cried joyfully. "You will see. There will be, as it were, a shower of roses!"

A shower of roses! What did this mean? wondered my godmother. And so did Pauline and Celine. But soon I was uttering an equally strange statement, and this one in the presence of several Sisters. On July 25 I was asked if I would look down on my friends from Heaven.

"No," I replied. *"I will come down!"*

While waiting for death to put an end to my suffering, I thought very often of Leonie in the Visitation monastery in Caen and of the two missionaries who had been given to me as spiritual brothers. On July 17 I had managed to write a farewell letter to Leonie, now known in religion as Sister Frances Therese. Then I turned my attention to the two missionaries. One was already in China, risking his life every day to win souls to Christ. The other was yet at the Seminary, still a bit fearful of the work awaiting him in Africa and very distressed at the news that my death was expected at any moment.

I tried to comfort this young student with these lines:

> "When my brother sets out for Africa, I shall follow him not only in thought and in prayer. I shall be always with him, and his faith will know well how to discern the presence of a little sister that Jesus has given

> him to be his helper not only during two short years, but till the end of his life..."

One day Pauline came to me with a request. By now she had read the various chapters of my book, and had enjoyed them very much. But there was one place where she felt some changes could be made. Did I feel strong enough to read over what I had written, then make these changes? Quickly I assured my "Little Mother" that I would be glad to do what I could, and presently the manuscript was brought to me.

It was not hard to make the changes, but when Pauline returned to the Infirmary my eyes were wet with tears.

"You've been crying," she said reproachfully. "The work was too much for you."

I shook my head. There are tears of pain, but there are also tears of joy, and mine were definitely tears of joy. Suddenly I had realized that God intended that the little manuscript before me should do a great deal of good. Countless thousands would read it and begin to follow my Little Way.

For a long moment I looked at Pauline. Then I gave a deep sigh. "I know it!" I whispered happily. *"Some day everyone is going to love me!"*

CHAPTER 15

GOD CALLS ME TO HEAVEN

I RECEIVED the Last Sacraments on July 30. By now everyone was convinced that death would be only a matter of hours, for I was suffering intensely. Every breath was a torment. I could scarcely bear the pain, even though faith told me that many poor sinners were being helped because I was offering this pain for them.

"But in the end Sister Therese will have an easy death," said one of the nuns. "Wait and see. It will be just as though she fell asleep."

I did not agree. To spare my sisters sorrow, I would have been glad to have an easy death, but my ever-present thought was that my own wishes did not matter. Long ago I had asked God to take away my will and let only His Will be manifest in me. Besides, there was the death of Christ on the Cross. Had it been beautiful, or easy? No—it had been bloody and agonizing. For the sake of sinners, the Heavenly Father had allowed His Son to undergo the most dreadful sufferings. Upheld by grace, I now would try to imitate Christ to the last.

Contrary to everyone's expectations, I still had several more weeks to live. On August 1 Pauline told me once more how pleased she was with my book. It was truly *The Story of a Soul.* Later on she hoped to have it read to the community and published, too. Perhaps some of the Sisters would object to my poor little words being given such a wide audience, but she felt that should not matter. The whole world ought to know about my Little Way.

As she was speaking, something prompted me to offer this advice:

"My Mother, after my death the manuscript should not be spoken of to anyone until it is published. If you do otherwise, or if you delay the publication, the Devil will set many snares for you in order to hinder God's good work . . . a work that is very important. . ."

Yes, I was convinced that my book was a good one, not owing to any merit of mine but solely to the assistance which the Heavenly Father had given me. He had inspired me to write knowingly of His goodness and mercy because He wished that souls everywhere should love Him as I loved Him. They were not to be afraid of His Will.

Presently I reflected upon a statement made by one of the Sisters. She had said that it was easy for me to have confidence in God because I had never offended Him by mortal sin. But what about others, people living in the world who had committed all manner of serious offenses? Surely it would be hard for them to be as little children, to fly into the arms of the Heavenly Father in complete confidence that He would forgive them? I had replied to her question with these words, which I later inserted in the story of my life:

> "I know that I should lose nothing of my confidence even if I had on my conscience every crime that could be committed. Heartbroken with repentance, I would throw myself into the arms of my Saviour. I know that He loves the Prodigal Son; I have heard His words to Saint Mary Magdalen . . . No one could make me fear, for I know what to believe concerning His love and His mercy. I know that all that multitude of sins would disappear in an instant, as a drop of water cast into a flaming furnace."

"These words and all the others I have written are true!" I told myself happily. "Dear God, thank You for helping me to write them!"

For several months I had not been able to be with the novices. The Prioress had declared that they were not to bother me with their troubles and doubts, for I was not strong enough to speak more than was necessary. But one August day a little group was allowed to come to the Infirmary. For the time being I was not suffering quite as much as usual. Possibly one visit from my friends would not hurt me.

The young Sisters gathered about my bed, their eyes wide with sympathy. What a change sickness had wrought in Sister Therese of the Child Jesus! She was so thin, so weak! Finally one of them spoke:

"You are always seeking to be like a little child," she said, "but won't you tell us what must be done to obtain Eternal Life?"

I smiled at the question. When a person gives up his pride, when he becomes a little child in spirit, he has taken the most important step toward obtaining Eternal Life. After all I had told them, why didn't the novices understand that *childhood* and *Heaven* go together? But I hid my thoughts, and patiently tried to give one more explanation of my Little Way.

" 'Remaining little' means that we recognize our nothingness," I said, "that we await everything from the goodness of God *as a little child expects everything from its father*, that we are not anxious about anything and that we do not think about collecting spiritual riches. Even among the poor, a child receives what is necessary while he is still small; once he is grown up, his father will no longer keep him but tells him to work and support himself. It was to avoid hearing this that I have put away every desire to grow up, for I feel incapable of earning my livelihood, which is Eternal Life. That is why I have remained little; my only care has been to gather flowers of love and sacrifice and to offer them to God for His good pleasure."

The novices were silent for a moment. Then one remarked a bit doubtfully that many people might misunderstand my words. To become a little child in spirit, to put oneself in the arms of the Heavenly Father and seek everything from Him—why, surely there is an element of laziness in this!

"Oh, no!" I hastened to explain. "When you are in the arms of the Heavenly Father, you are really in a watchtower. You can see many new and wonderful ways of pleasing Him. Ever since I placed myself there, I have been like a watchman on the lookout for the enemy from the highest turret of a fortified castle; nothing escapes my vigilance... I am often surprised at my own clear-sightedness."

Then I gave one more definition of holiness:

"Sanctity does not consist in the practice of certain exercises of piety but in a disposition of the heart which makes us humble and little in the arms of God, conscious of our weakness but confiding—unhesitatingly—in His Fatherly Goodness."

As the days passed, I became steadily weaker. Celine, now Sister Genevieve of the Holy Face, had been appointed Assistant Infirmarian, and she spent her nights in a cell adjoining the Infirmary. She did everything to help me, and I was glad to have her near, but at the same time I was grieved because I knew that my coughing spells disturbed her. Presently I asked the Blessed Virgin to let these spells occur in the daytime only, so that Celine might be able to get her much needed rest.

"But if you do not hear me, I shall love you still more," I said.

The Devil was very busy these days, and soon the temptations against faith grew even worse than before. One day, as I lay gazing out of the window at the beautiful summer sky, one of the Sisters made an effort to comfort me.

"Soon you will be up there, beyond that blue sky," she said.

I smiled, but later I confessed to Pauline that the Sister's words had brought me no cheer. The sky was beautiful, yes, but somehow I could not see beyond it. Only the lovely color caught my eye. Every day Heaven seemed to be more hopelessly closed to me.

As August gave place to September, greater temptations came my way. One night my grief of soul was almost too much to bear, and I begged the Infirmarian to sprinkle Holy Water on my bed.

"I do not see the Devil, but I feel his presence!" I cried. "He is tormenting me! He holds me with an iron hand! He prevents me from getting the slightest relief! He increases my pain in order to lead me to despair...."

Quickly the Infirmarian brought the Holy Water and sprinkled it generously about the bed. She also lighted a blessed candle.

"Pray," she urged gently. "Have confidence."

I sighed. "Oh, Sister, I cannot pray! I can only look at the Blessed Virgin and say 'Jesus'! I know I do not suffer for myself but for another soul... and the Devil is so displeased!"

The Infirmarian, much impressed with these words, remained with me for several minutes. To the best of my ability I tried to tell her how necessary it is to pray for the dying. Few people realize how furiously the Devil fights to drag souls to Hell, all during our life but most especially at the hour of our death. He knows that now his last chance has come, and so he tries his best to sow discouragement in the human heart. Our past sins, long ago forgiven, are dragged forth to stand in a new and ugly light. The very thought of God is torture, for He is now revealed as a Creator Who cannot abide the slightest imperfection. He is shown as a God of Justice, without love, and the poor sufferer trembles at the thought of the punishment which is in store for him. All this is readily accomplished in the suffering soul, for the Devil has enormous powers. He is really an angel, with an angel's keen intelligence, and he well knows how to frighten a weak human being.

Even as I reflected upon this, and struggled hard not to give way before the Devil's onslaughts, peace suddenly flooded my soul. I knew once more that although God may be a God of Justice, He is also a God of Mercy. The blessing of His Holy Church was in the candle burning beside my bed, in the

Holy Water that had been sprinkled about me. The Devil knew this, too, and he had fled from the Strength that must always be greater than his.

On September 14 someone brought me a rose. I was holding my crucifix at the time, and as a mark of love for Our Lord I touched each of the Five Wounds with the fragrant petals. Later some of these petals fell to the floor. Celine would have swept them up and thrown them away, but suddenly I astonished her with these words:

"Gather up these petals, but do not lose one of them. Later on, they will enable you to give pleasure."

Marie and Pauline were present, and their eyes filled with wonder at my comment. What did I mean?

I knew what I meant. Some day many people were going to read my book, *The Story of a Soul,* and see God in a new light. They would discover that He was not only their Judge but their Father, and thousands of souls would forget their fear of Him, of His Will in their regard. They would joyfully set about their most important task, that of achieving holiness, by becoming as little children. Because I, poor and weak though I was, had been chosen to teach souls that the surest way to Heaven is the Little Way, these rose petals which I had touched would be treated as very precious objects.

Two weeks later I was still alive and still suffering in mind and body. But on September 29, at about nine o'clock in the evening, there came a sign which seemed to indicate that my death was now very close at hand. Celine was with me when a turtle dove appeared from out the autumn twilight and perched on the window sill near my bed. It stayed there for several minutes, cooing gently. As we watched this unexpected little visitor, those beautiful lines from the Canticle of Canticles flashed through our minds:

> "Behold, my Beloved speaketh to me. Arise, make haste, my love, my dove, my beautiful one, and come. For winter is now past, the rain is over and gone. The flowers have appeared in our land, the time of pruning is come. The voice of the turtle is heard in our land. The fig tree hath put forth her green figs; the vines in flower yield their sweet smell. Arise, my love, my beautiful one, and come."

Yes—Christ was inviting me, a little one of His Church, to the never-ending springtime which is Heaven!

The suffering was not quite over, however. All that night and all the next day, September 30, I gasped and struggled for breath. I was consumed with fever. Never had I thought it possible to suffer so much, never, never! The only meaning of such suffering could be that since I had made myself a victim for others, God was accepting my offering in its entirety.

My sisters scarcely left my side, or Mother Mary Gonzaga. About three o'clock in the afternoon the

NEVER HAD I THOUGHT IT POSSIBLE TO SUFFER SO MUCH!

suffering became so intense that I felt I could not bear it. I extended my arms in the form of a cross and looked beseechingly at the Prioress.

"Oh, my Mother! Present me to the Blessed Virgin without delay! Prepare me to die well!"

The Prioress soothed me as best she could, then showed me a little image of Our Lady of Mount Carmel. She reminded me that I had always understood and practiced humility and that God is merciful toward those who have made themselves small.

I drew comfort from these words. Yes, I had never sought anything but the truth. From childhood I had understood humility of heart. Besides, was it not written in Psalm 75 that at the end of the world the Lord will arise to save the meek and humble of the earth? It was written not that He should come to *judge* but that He should come to *save.*

With a great effort I let Mother Mary Gonzaga understand that I was not afraid of God or of what He had in store for me. The temptations against faith were still present, but I was fighting them with every ounce of my strength.

"I do not repent of having surrendered myself to Love," I said.

The hours passed, and I lingered on. Some minutes after seven o'clock the Prioress dismissed most of the Sisters who had been praying about my bed. Hearing their departure, I looked up.

"Mother, am I not going to die?"

"Yes, my child. But perhaps the good God wishes to prolong your suffering for a few hours...."

I sighed and clutched my crucifix. "Well, then, let it be so. I would not want to suffer less."

Slowly the seconds ticked away. By now I could scarcely breathe. Suddenly I looked once more on the crucifix. Had the time finally come for me to offer my last prayer on earth? Yes, I told myself. It has come, and with all my strength I gasped out the simple words:

"Oh, I love Him! My God . . . I . . . love . . . You!"

Then I closed my eyes, and my head fell back against the pillow.

Instantly Mother Mary Gonzaga was convinced that I was dead. She ordered the bell rung to call the community to my side. But when the Sisters reached the Infirmary, they found that I was still alive. Quietly they knelt about me, praying, praying, praying. Then everyone present witnessed a most extraordinary sight. Suddenly I had opened my eyes, had raised myself in bed, and now I was gazing joyfully at a point a little above the Blessed Virgin's statue.

"What is it?" they wondered silently. "Sister Therese doesn't look tired and sick any more. She looks positively beautiful!"

Yes, the dreadful sufferings were over now, and God was granting me a glimpse of Heaven. The vision was so full of glory, so wonderful, that I could not help reflecting it in my own poor body. For more than a minute I gazed at the beautiful sight, utterly unable to speak. Then the summons came. God was satisfied with the little servant who had labored for Him on this earth for twenty-four years and nine months. Now her reward was at hand.

As my head fell back a second time on the pillow, the nuns redoubled their prayers. Sister Therese of the Child Jesus and of the Holy Face was dead!

Dead? Oh, no! I was just beginning to live. Had I not been inspired to say, many weeks before, that I WOULD SPEND MY HEAVEN IN DOING GOOD UPON EARTH? Yes—and now the time had come. It was September 30, 1897, but until the end of the world I would work for souls. I would come down to them when they called upon me. I would let fall a shower of roses—the fragrant flowers of God's grace—with a generous hand. And *The Story of a Soul*, my book, would carry the happy message of my Little Way to every corner of the earth!

New York City
Feast of Corpus Christi
June 8, 1944

NOTE

When this book first went to press (February, 1950), two sisters of Saint Therese of the Child Jesus were still living in the Carmel of Lisieux: Pauline (Mother Agnes of Jesus) and Celine (Sister Genevieve of the Holy Face). Both these sisters have since gone to their eternal reward.

The dates of their deaths and the death dates of the other relatives of the Saint who figure in this story are as follows:

Aunt Celine Guerin—February 13, 1900.
Marie Guerin (Sister Mary of the Eucharist)—April 14, 1905.
Uncle Isidore Guerin—September 28, 1909.
Jane Guerin La Néele—April 25, 1938.
Marie (Sister Mary of the Sacred Heart)—January 19, 1940.
Leonie (Sister Frances Therese)—June 16, 1941.
Pauline (Mother Agnes of Jesus)—1951.
Celine (Sister Genevieve of the Holy Face)—1959.

—*The Publishers,* 1991

PRAYER TO ST. THERESE OF THE CHILD JESUS FOR THE CONVERSION OF RUSSIA

O LOVING and compassionate Saint, deign to comfort our Russian brethren, the victims of a long and cruel persecution of the Christian name. Obtain for them perseverance in the Faith and progress in the love of God and their neighbor, along with great confidence in the most holy Mother of God. Prepare for them holy priests who shall make reparation for the blasphemies and sacrileges committed against the Holy Eucharist. Grant that angelic purity may once more flourish among them, especially in the young, as well as every Christian virtue, so that this noble people, being delivered from all slavery and returning freely to the one Fold which the loving Heart of the Risen Christ entrusted to St. Peter and his successors, may at length taste the joy of glorifying the Father and the Son and the Holy Spirit in the fellowship of the holy Catholic Church. Amen.